D1608064

Imagine being able to ask Charlotte Ford, Mrs. Robert F. Wagner, Mrs. William Fine, and Governor Hugh Carey's Special Assistant Isabelle Leeds for their personal recommendations of what to do and where to shop in New York. That's what this unique directory lets you do—benefit from the personal recommendations of four of New York's most prominent women, whose appreciation of style, quality, service and value is well known.

The authors have picked out the places where *they* go—to buy clothes, furniture, unusual gifts; to get a suit altered or dry-cleaned, jewelry designed, an apartment decorated, hair styled, parties catered. As practical as it is chic, their clever guide—complete with store hours, addresses, phone numbers—is filled with the kind of inside information a visitor or less experienced New Yorker might never unearth on her own.

Charlotte, Isabelle, Phyllis & Susan's

N.Y., N.Y.

A Woman's Guide to Shops, Services & Restaurants

Charlotte, Isabelle, Phyllis & Susan's

N.Y., N.Y.

Charlotte Ford,
Isabelle Russek Leeds,
Phyllis Cerf Wagner,
Susan Payson Fine

Random House New York

Acknowledgment
We are grateful to Carol Sherman who typed, who checked, who
cheered us on.
    Our thanks, also, to Peter Rodgers for designing the back of the
jacket, and to Richard Davis for taking the photograph.

Library of Congress Cataloging in Publication Data
Main entry under title:
Charlotte, Isabelle, Phyllis & Susan's N.Y., N.Y.
1. Shopping—New York (City)—Directories.
I. Ford, Charlotte, 1941–
HF5429.5N5C5   380.1'025'7471   77-6004
ISBN 0-394-73333-9

Manufactured in the United States of America
9 8 7 6 5 4 3 2
First Edition

to N.Y., N.Y.,
our favorite town

Contents

Introduction

To a cartographer, "The Big Apple," New York City, is made up of five slices: the Bronx, Brooklyn, Manhattan, Queens and Staten Island, too. It covers a land area of 25,000 square acres, has a population of 7 1/2 million and is one of the great metropolitan centers of the world. The pulse beat of this huge metropolis is the island of Manhattan—known to the world as New York, New York. It is in Manhattan that everything happens: Wall Street houses the great financial district; Seventh Avenue is the fashion capital of America; Madison Avenue is synonymous with advertising; major national and international corporations are neighbors on a five-block strip of Park Avenue; the headquarters of TV networks are clustered around the Avenue of the Americas; Broadway connotes the Theater; United Nations Plaza regularly plays host to the world's leading diplomats.

But Manhattan is also just plain home to the four authors of this book: Charlotte, Isabelle, Phyllis and Susan. We now live within four blocks of one another and, collectively, we have lived in New York, New York, for eighty-seven years. Like the other 7 1/2 million with whom we share residency, we have a certain twenty-block radius that is "our town." It is centered on Manhattan's East Side, which is politically known as the "silk-stocking district" and is in the heart of one of the world's most concentrated and most fashionable shopping and cultural areas. This book is about that New York. What we four luxury-loving persons set out to do was to tell you about the shops we shop, the restaurants we frequent and the services we rely on.

This is a personal and opinionated directory that represents our taste, our style and our demands for quality, service and value. It is a guide to what we think is great in the better-known places as well as in all the little oases we haunt which a visitor or even a less-experienced New Yorker might never unearth. Part of the fun in writing this book was the opportunity it gave us to thank the people who really care about the service or product they provide. We have listed others whom we patronize only because they have something we want or need and can't get elsewhere.

Part of the excitement of Manhattan is that it is an ever-changing scene, with its buildings constantly being torn down and rebuilt. In fact, one visitor commented that "New York will be a lovely place if they ever get it finished." We hope they never do. Yet this state of flux means that by the time you read this, a great new boutique may have moved into our neighborhood—too late to be mentioned, or an old favorite may have gone out of business or changed its location. At press time, however, all the shops recommended in this book were in business and at the addresses we have listed, and they are *the* places we like the most. So follow us to them and avoid the frustrations and unnecessary footsteps common to the random shopper.

Our greatest reward will be if we can make *our* New York, New York, *your* wonderful town.

Street Guide

It is easy to find one's way around our Manhattan. Roughly, it runs between 34th and 96th Streets and lies between two rivers. The intervening streets are consecutively numbered. You cross from river to river on these streets; this is called going "crosstown." You travel "uptown" and "downtown" on Avenues. Going toward 34th Street you're heading toward what is called "downtown," and heading toward 96th Street is described as going "uptown."

Our island is bisected by Fifth Avenue, which is the demarcation of what is known as the East Side and the West Side. Every building between Fifth Avenue and the Hudson River has a West Side address, while those between Fifth Avenue and the East River have an East Side address. The direction of traffic for most streets and avenues is one way, with the odd numbered streets mostly going West and the even numbered streets mostly going East. The numbers on the buildings get larger as they near the rivers; the building numbers on avenues get higher as you go uptown. New Yorkers still say "Sixth Avenue" even though its name was changed to "Avenue of the Americas" years ago.

What to Wear When

While it's not quite true that if you don't like our New York weather you need only to wait a minute, our temperature does rise and fall enough to make life interesting. As reported by Pan Am World *Horizons*, our average temperatures are: January 33°, February 33°, March 40°, April 52°, May 62°, June 72°, July 77°, August 76°, September 69°, October 59°, November 48°, December 35°.

The temperature and city dirt dictate the weight and color of our clothes, but we also have fad-shionable idiosyncrasies. No matter what the thermometer reads, modish New Yorkers never don their summer apparel until after Memorial Day. Then the cottons and silks generally worn are in dark colors—both printed and solid (though in recent years lighter shades have been showing up in June and July). Nearly all our dresses have jackets or long sleeves to protect us from the icy air conditioning that prevails in restaurants, offices, theaters and other public places. Gentlemen wear ties and jackets to work, to restaurants and on the street. No New Yorker would ever be caught on the sidewalks of our town in a pair of white shoes—they're just not practical; neither are white suits, pants, or coats for men, but ladies do venture out in them in the evening. For shopping, running errands or going to the hairdresser women wear tailored pants suits or blue jeans, tastefully accessorized with fancy belts, silk shirts, handsome shoes and jackets. Although tailored pants suits and jeans are universally permissible, they are not worn by women to elegant restaurants for either lunch or dinner. Silk pajama outfits, on the other hand, are becoming almost a year-round uniform in the evening at restaurants and at private and public events. Suits and short, dressy dresses of silks, satins, velvets, laces and chiffons are referred to by salespersons as "theater suits" and "restaurant dresses" respectively, and that's where they are mostly worn.

Opening nights for musical shows, opera, concerts and ballet are nearly always "black tie" events for those with orchestra seats and boxes; other nights, one wears a restaurant dress or a theater suit.

The "black tie" season for men (except for large public dinners) virtually comes to an end on Memorial Day and doesn't reappear until October 1st. Women wear long dresses all year round. People dining "duo" in restaurants rarely wear formal attire unless they are on their way to or from a "black tie" event.

Come Labor Day, the typical New Yorker puts away her cotton dresses, no matter what the temperature. Fur jackets come out in October, but full-length fur coats are rarely seen before November 15th or after April 15th. Spring coats and suits work in April, May, September and October. Few New Yorkers, men or women, wear hats or gloves except for warmth. Truthfully, most of us dress any way we want to—except when going to the grandest places.

Charlotte, Isabelle, Phyllis & Susan's

N.Y., N.Y.

A Woman's Guide to Shops, Services & Restaurants

Air Cargo

When time is of the essence and cost is a secondary consideration, special packages—small or large—can be sped from door
to door via one of the following services.

There are catches: unless you have a charge account with
the cargo company, you must prepay. Charges are determined
by size and weight. If it's a trunk you're trying to weigh and
your only scale is of the bathroom variety—good luck. Emery
Air Freight suggests you first weigh the trunk, and then each
item as it's packed. They also point out that they will promise
a date of pickup but not the specific hour. Because of these
drawbacks, we are apt to use these services only when shipping
large items. You can send a hundred-pound package from
New York to Miami for about $75.

AIR EXPRESS INTERNATIONAL / pickup and delivery service:
  632–3526

EMERY AIR FREIGHT / 995–6411; 995–6375; 656–7373

FLYING TIGER LINE / JFK: 632–1111;
  Newark: 201–961–3600

Airlines

See page 210.

Alterations

If you're finicky about well-fitted clothes, you'll find that having clothes altered in a department store is usually time consuming and expensive, and the end result is not always satisfactory. Most boutiques don't do alterations at all. As far as we're concerned, if clothes do not feel right, they simply don't look right. Our answer is to have our own seamstress come in to sew or to use a good tailor in the neighborhood.

ANN'S / 1020 Lexington Avenue between 72nd and 73rd Streets
Monday through Friday 7:00 to 7:00 / 249-1372

Anne's is one of those friendly old-fashioned places that word-of-mouth has passed on over the years from friend to friend. There's nothing fancy about the premises—it's a second-floor walk-up with one small dressing room—but the minute you talk to Anne you know your clothes are in good hands. She alters and fits men's, women's and children's clothes and anything else that needs a stitch in time quickly and inexpensively.

POTISMAN'S TAILORS, INC. / 25 East 63rd Street between
Madison and Park Avenues / Monday through Saturday 9:00 to
6:00 / 838-3370

Potisman cleans and presses women's and men's clothing, and on the side they are terrific tailors. Perfect for small alterations.

FRED WINKLER / 137 East 61st Street between Lexington and
Park Avenues / Monday through Saturday 7:30 to 6:00 / 838-7757

This proverbial "little tailor" is for both men and women. He'll turn up or let down hems and cuffs, in a reasonable amount of time and at a fair rate.

Antique Dealers

The United States Custom Law classifies an antique as any object made prior to 1830. New York teems with merchandise of this vintage, ranging from signed FFF (Fine French Furniture) to Chinese Chippendale to Early American. However, "antique" has come to mean anything that has been previously owned, including the memorabilia from grandparents' attics. This kind of "antique" can also be found in New York, making it the eclectic collector's dream.

A LA VIEILLE RUSSIE, INC. / 781 Fifth Avenue at 59th Street
Monday through Friday 9:30 to 5:30 / 752-1727

For the Fabergé connoisseur this is *the* place to shop. Unless you have a Tsar's ransom to spend for these treasures from Imperial Russia, content yourself with looking in its windows.

*ANTIQUE CENTER OF AMERICA / 415 East 53rd Street
between First Avenue and Sutton Place / Tuesday through
Saturday 10:30 to 5:30, Sunday noon to 6:00 / 486–0941*

The Antique Center of America is New York's oldest version of the
Marche aux Puces in Paris. This collection of dozens of shops under one
roof is surely the largest "garage sale" ever. There's lots of junk, but an
occasional bargain can be had if you know your stuff. Wandering around
from vendor to vendor is a pleasant way to wile away a lazy Sunday
afternoon, especially if you want to fill in a collection of glass, dishes,
antique jewelry, silver or porcelain.

*ANTIQUE COMPANY OF NEW YORK (also: Antique
Porcelain Company) 48 East 57th Street between Madison and
Park Avenues / Monday through Saturday 9:00 to 6:00 / 758–2363*

If there's a more expensive porcelain shop than this one, we haven't seen
it. It has, for example, a very rare selection of $100,000 dinner services,
if that's what you happen to be in the market for. The collection of
porcelain is beautiful, but here we are mostly "lookers" not "buyers."

*SARAH POTTER CONOVER, INC. / 17 East 64th Street
between Fifth and Madison Avenues / Monday through Friday
10:00 to 5:00, Saturday 10:00 to 4:00 / 861–0515*

This small shop specializes in fine porcelain, though it also carries a few
choice pieces of furniture. A good address to ferret out the perfect
ashtray, candy dish or vitrine filler for the home. Expensive, but
reasonably so.

*FRENCH & COMPANY / 17 East 65th Street between Fifth and
Madison Avenues / Monday through Friday 10:00 to 5:00,
Saturday by appointment / 535–3330*

This well-established company is known for the very best in French and
English 18th-century furniture, although it is also possible to buy a
Picasso or Rodin here. In addition, they have a fine selection of 16th-
and 17th-century bronzes, antique tapestries, carpets and rugs. This is a
shop for serious collectors only.

INCURABLE COLLECTOR / 36 East 57th Street between
Madison and Park Avenues / Monday through Friday 9:30 to 5:30,
Saturday 10:00 to 4:00 / 755–0140

If you are an incurable collector who constantly buys things to take
home to repair at a later date, this shop will be your salvation because it
has done all the work for you. Here you will find once-injured pieces of
china, silver and furniture (mostly from the 18th century) that have been
repaired and polished back to mint condition. (Keep in mind as you
marvel that polishing time and 57th Street overhead are reflected in the
purchase price.)

JOSEPH LOMBARDO / 120 East 55th Street between Lexington
and Park Avenues / Monday through Friday 9:00 to 5:00
753–9665

Joseph Lombardo has the best (and probably had N.Y.'s first) Oriental
woven cane-wrapped tables, in all sizes and shapes. They are lacquered to
order in the color of your choice. Perhaps it is because these tables are
alcohol-proof (albeit vacuum-cleaner-chip prone) that accounts for their
position smack in the center of living rooms up and down Park Avenue.
Also, there is a good selection of small pieces of French furniture and
porcelain. You won't get all of this chic for nothing.

MANHATTAN ART AND ANTIQUES CENTER / 1050
Second Avenue between 55th and 56th Streets / Monday through
Saturday 10:30 to 6:30, Sunday noon to 6:00 / 355–4400

This is one of those multifloor, multidealer antique marts with art
galleries as well as antique shops. There is good merchandise here,
displayed to best advantage because of the spaciousness.

D. M. & P. MANHEIM / 46 East 57th Street between Madison
and Park Avenues / Monday through Friday 9:30 to 5:30, Saturday
9:30 to 4:00 / closed Saturday Memorial Day through September
758–2986

A mind-boggling collection of old English pottery, porcelain and
enamels, with a few pieces from China. If you collect Battersea boxes or
Chelsea ware, this is a not-to-be-missed stop. Like all of 57th Street, it's
expensive.

NORMAND MAXON / 167 East 61st Street between Lexington and Third Avenues / Monday through Friday 9:00 to 5:00, Saturday by appointment / 759-5471

The sign on the door says *to the trade only* (which means you should be accompanied by a decorator), but if you knock and smile politely, you may be permitted to browse and buy. Maxon's collection is very eclectic and "special," i.e., it will not appeal to every taste. But try him for exotic Orientalia, exquisite Lalique and boxes covered in antique fabric. A few small bibelots can be had at bargain prices, but in general exotica is expensive.

NESLE INC. / 151 East 57th Street between Lexington and Third Avenues / Monday through Friday 9:00 to 5:00 / 755-0515

If you have a room with a very high ceiling and your heart is set on a real crystal chandelier, Nesle's is the place to find the most sparkling "hangers" in town. They also offer other decorative items, including rococo urns, vases, sconces and stands. A rich selection in rich taste at rich prices.

PRICE GLOVER / 57 East 57th Street between Madison and Park Avenues / third floor / Monday through Friday 10:00 to 5:00, Saturday 10:00 to 4:30 / 486-9767

The emphasis here is on 18th-century English pewter and pottery. They also have furniture, paintings and other decorative items. You won't have to elbow your way through lots of other customers to see what there is to see in this shop, but you will need to be enterprising to negotiate the self-service elevator that takes you there. Expensive, but you'll get what you pay for.

JAMES ROBINSON / 12 East 57th Street between Fifth and Madison Avenues / Monday through Friday 10:00 to 6:00, Saturday 11:00 to 5:00 / 752-6166

Specialists in 17th-, 18th- and early 19th-century English hallmark silver, antique jewelry and complete sets of rare porcelain dinner services. For stylish gifts and less expensive items look upstairs at the Victorian potpourri; the items and prices downstairs are more likely to suit the purses of doting rich aunts and uncles, and Middle Eastern sheiks.

ROSENBERG & STIEBEL / 32 East 57th Street between Fifth and Madison Avenues / Monday through Friday 10:00 to 5:00 753–4368

A small but well-known antique dealer who purveys 18th-century FFFurniture, *objects d'art* and a selection of Old Master paintings to those who collect the best.

STAIR & COMPANY / 59 East 57th Street between Madison and Park Avenues / Monday through Friday 9:30 to 5:30, Saturday 10:00 to 3:00 / 355–7620

Stair & Company's name stands for quality. Good interior decorators with clients searching for authentic antique English furniture and appropriate accessories find this retail store an important source. The stock obviously varies, but generally a good number of tables, breakfronts, chairs and side pieces are on hand. If you want an excuse to go in and look around, ask about their special furniture wax, which they will happily sell you to preserve the finish on your own prized pieces.

FREDERICK VICTORIA / 154 East 55th Street between Lexington and Third Avenues / Monday through Friday 9:00 to 4:30 / 755–2549

Mr. Victoria, one of New York's most respected antique dealers, is among the first stops for many top decorators with clients in tow. For here are six floors chock-a-block full of paneled rooms, furniture and accessories. Whether it's the wood with which to build an armoire, an unusual old side chair or a charming bibelot for a table top, the choice here is varied, the quality fine, and the price high.

S. WYLER, INC. / 713 Madison Avenue at 63rd Street / Monday through Saturday 9:00 to 5:30 / 838–1910

If it's fish forks and knives, teething rings, old picture frames or other silver sentimentalia you're after, it's there. But the Wylers' real specialty is antique silver and fine porcelain. The merchandise is well displayed and the salespeople are helpful. This is not Tiffany & Co., but the Wyler label is still highly acceptable to name-droppers.

Art Dealers and Galleries

For New York art lovers, Saturday is traditionally "Doing the Galleries Day." The center of today's art world runs across 57th Street, from Park Avenue to Sixth Avenue, and up, down, and around Madison Avenue; beginning in the 800 block, it reaches full force in the 900 to 1000 blocks. Here galleries are filled with everything from Old Masters to contemporary artwork.

The *New York Times* on Friday and Saturday carries a listing of many New York galleries and dealers and gives details of various artists' shows. The galleries we like and have bought from are listed below. If you're interested in seeing more, we suggest the *Art Dealers Association of America Handbook* as a reputable guide. For this free booklet, telephone 644–7150, or write to Art Dealers Association of America, 575 Madison Avenue, New York, New York 10021.

ACQUAVELLA ART GALLERIES, INC. / 18 East 79th Street between Fifth and Madison Avenues / Monday through Saturday 10:00 to 5:00 / closed Saturday Memorial Day through Labor Day / 734–6300

Old Master, Impressionist, Post-Impressionist and contemporary paintings.

LEO CASTELLI GALLERY / 4 East 77th Street between Fifth and Madison Avenues / Monday through Saturday 10:00 to 6:00 288–3202

Vanguard graphics and photography.

TIBOR DE NAGY GALLERY, INC. / 29 West 57th Street between Fifth and Sixth Avenues / Tuesday through Saturday 10:00 to 5:30 / 421–3780

Contemporary art, both abstract and representational.

RICHARD L. FEIGEN & COMPANY / 900 Park Avenue at
79th Street / Monday through Saturday 9:00 to 6:00 / 628–0700

Paintings of 15th- to 20th-century masters.

DAVID FINDLAY / 984 Madison Avenue between 76th and 77th
Streets / Tuesday through Saturday 10:00 to 5:00 / 249–2909

European and American paintings and sculpture of the 19th and 20th
centuries.

FISCHBACH GALLERY / 29 West 57th Street between Fifth and
Sixth Avenues / Monday through Saturday 10:00 to 5:30
759–2345

Twentieth-century American painting, sculpture and drawings.

STEPHEN HAHN GALLERY / 817 Fifth Avenue at 63rd Street
Monday through Friday 10:30 to 5:00 / by appointment
759–6645

French paintings of the 19th and 20th centuries.

MARTHA JACKSON WEST / 521 West 57th Street between
Tenth and Eleventh Avenues / Tuesday through Saturday 10:00 to
5:30 / 586–4200

International contemporary paintings, sculpture and graphics.

SIDNEY JANIS GALLERY / 6 West 57th Street between Fifth
and Sixth Avenues / Monday through Saturday 10:00 to 5:00
586–0110

Three generations of modern art from Cubism to Pop to Photo-Realism.

M. KNOEDLER & CO. / 19 East 70th Street between Fifth and
Madison Avenues / Tuesday through Friday 9:30 to 5:30, Saturday
10:00 to 6:00 / 628–0400

Old Masters, 19th- and 20th-century European and American paintings
and sculpture.

PIERRE MATISSE GALLERY CORP. / *41 East 57th Street at Madison Avenue / Monday through Friday 10:00 to 5:00 355–6269*

Contemporary paintings and sculpture.

MULTIPLES, INC. / *55 East 80th Street between Madison and Park Avenues / Monday through Saturday 10:00 to 6:00 / 988–2200*

Contemporary prints and editions.

NEWHOUSE GALLERIES / *19 East 66th Street between Fifth and Madison Avenues / Monday through Friday 9:30 to 5:00, Saturday 9:30 to noon / 879–2700*

Paintings from the 17th and 18th centuries.

PACE GALLERY / *32 East 57th Street between Madison and Park Avenues / Tuesday through Friday 9:30 to 5:30, Saturday 10:00 to 6:00 / 421–3292*

Twentieth-century painting, sculpture and graphics.

PERLS GALLERY / *1016 Madison Avenue between 78th and 79th Streets / Tuesday through Saturday 10:00 to 5:30 / 472–3200*

Paintings and sculpture by 20th-century masters.

PAUL ROSENBERG & CO. / *20 East 79th Street between Fifth and Madison Avenues / Monday through Friday 9:30 to 5:30 472–1134*

French paintings of the 19th and 20th centuries; contemporary American and European paintings and sculpture.

WILDENSTEIN AND COMPANY / *19 East 64th Street between Fifth and Madison Avenues / Monday through Saturday 10:00 to 5:30 / 879–0500*

Old Masters and Impressionists.

Artist Supplies

EMPIRE ARTISTS MATERIAL / 851 Lexington Avenue between 64th and 65th Streets / Monday through Friday 8:30 to 6:00, Saturday 9:00 to 5:00 / 737–5002

Suppliers of paints, canvases stretched to order, boards, sketchbooks, paper and all the other needs of an artist. The pleasant management is always willing to give personal attention and advice to budding Rembrandts. A wonderful place to get art framed (see page 158) or to buy large pads of newsprint for children's scribbles.

SAM FLAX / 551 Madison Avenue between 55th and 56th Streets Monday through Friday 9:30 to 6:00, Saturday 11:00 to 5:00 481–4747
55 East 55th Street between Madison and Park Avenues Monday through Friday 9:00 to 6:00, Saturday 11:00 to 5:00 481–4737

The Sam Flax stores provide fun for the amateur or beginner, but they also have a wide range of supplies for the pro. What F. A. O. Schwarz is for the toy connoisseur (adult or child), Sam Flax is for the artist (commercial or fine).

Auction Houses

Another area in which New York excels is the auction gallery. Along with dozens of smaller enterprises, we have the world's most renowned auctioneers—Sotheby Parke Bernet and Christie.

A word from the wise . . . Smart buyers or collectors always view the merchandise beforehand, check the estimates published in the auctioneer's catalogue and keep a top price firmly in mind.

The apocryphal story about adjusting your glasses and becoming the horrified owner of a $20,000 item is slightly exaggerated. Still, the amateur would be well advised to enlist the bidding aid of the readily available staff members.

CHRISTIE'S PARK AVENUE / Delmonico Hotel / 502 Park Avenue between 59th and 60th Streets / 826-2888

This auction house is a branch of the Christie's in London. Christie's sales, worldwide, topped $88,000,000 in 1976, a record that speaks for their expertise.

PARKE BERNET 84 (PB 84) 171 East 84th Street between Lexington and Third Avenues / exhibition hours: Monday 9:00 to 5:00, Tuesday 9:00 to 2:00, Saturday 10:00 to 6:00 / general information: 472-3583; recorded announcements on upcoming auctions: 472-3555

PB 84 is a subsidiary of Sotheby Parke Bernet. It performs essentially the same services, but only auctions goods estimated to bring in less than $1,000. If you're looking for secondhand goods, such as a club chair, carpet or pair of lamps, there are fantastic bargains here. The secret to successful buying is to know exactly what you're bidding on. The staff willingly helps neophytes with the auction procedures.

*SOTHEBY PARKE BERNET / 980 Madison Avenue between
76th and 77th Streets / viewing hours: Tuesday through Saturday
10:00 to 5:00; for sales schedules, check newspapers or recorded
information number / 472–3400; recorded announcements on
upcoming auctions: 472–3555*

Sotheby Parke Bernet appraises and auctions art, silver, jewelry,
porcelain, antiquities, tapestries, rugs, carpets, crystal, pewter, pottery,
paintings, prints, furniture, decorative items and real estate. This is
where great estates and great collections are put up for public sale. A
world-famous reputation for top prices is intimidating, and it's true that
at certain sales the objects are of museum quality and way out of range;
but, more often than you would suspect, the items on the block are
taken down at perfectly reasonable prices, especially if your heart isn't set
on what's currently considered fashionable. There are opportunities for
viewing two or three days before every sale, and whether you buy or not,
you can look over the collections on preview days and sit in on sale day.

Catalogues for all auctions are on sale at the main floor information
desk or by subscription through the mail.

(An aside: Bernet is pronounced to rhyme with *get.*)

Baby-Sitters

The best list of baby-sitting services was developed under the
auspices of the New York City Commission for the United
Nations and Consular Corps, to fill the needs of the large
diplomatic corps that is posted in N.Y., N.Y. We are happy
to pass it along to you, claiming full diplomatic immunity.

*AVALON NURSES AGENCY / 30 East 60th Street at Madison
Avenue / Monday through Sunday 8:00 A.M. to 8:30 P.M.
753–7278*

BABY SITTERS GUILD / *320 East 53rd Street between First and Second Avenues* / *Monday through Sunday 9:00 to 9:00* *751–8730*

BARNARD COLLEGE BABY SITTING SERVICE / *606 West 120th Street between Broadway and Claremont Avenue Monday through Friday 10:00 to 4:00* / *662–7676 (try to give as much notice as possible; same day not guaranteed)*

MARYMOUNT MANHATTAN COLLEGE STUDENT SERVICES / *221 East 71st Street between Second and Third Avenues* / *Monday through Friday 9:00 to 5:00* / *472–3800, extension 464*

STERN COLLEGE FOR WOMEN / *35th Street and Lexington Avenue* / *Monday through Friday 9:00 to 4:00* / *255–5600, extension 474*

GAIL TURNER NURSES REGISTRY / *138 East 61st Street between Lexington and Park Avenues* / *never closes* *838–5110*

Bakeries

See page 141.

Baskets

In primitive cultures around the world, baskets are still an important industry. Even in sophisticated urban environments such as N.Y., N.Y., basket weaving is a revived folk art. And little wonder, for the basket is no longer just a container. It is a collector's item, a wall sculpture, or a charming way to present food, gifts, flowers or almost anything else you want to amass. In fact, it's probably the most commonly used accessory today.

However you plan to weave baskets into your life style, you'll find a goodly supply in our town. In addition to the shops below, look for baskets in department stores, starting with Bloomingdale's—you may not need to go farther.

AZUMA / 666 Lexington Avenue between 55th and 56th Streets
  Monday through Saturday 10:00 to 9:00 / 752–0599
    251 East 86th Street between Second and Third Avenues
  Monday through Friday 10:00 to 10:00, Saturday 10:00 A.M. to
  10:30 P.M., Sunday 11:00 to 7:30 / 369–4928
    415 Fifth Avenue between 37th and 38th Streets / Monday
  through Saturday 10:00 to 6:30 / 889–4310

Copies of anything that's current in the basket line will turn up in one of the Azumas in a matter of days and be gone in a matter of hours. So if you see it and want it, buy it on sight. You're not apt to find it cheaper any place else.

CACHE-CACHE / 758 Madison Avenue between 65th and 66th
  Streets / Monday through Friday 10:00 to 5:30, Saturday 11:00 to
  5:00 / 744–6886; 744–7060

This attractive gift shop has lacquered baskets, along with many appropriate "tiskets and taskets" with which to fill them. For the wastebaskets, you can supply your own trash or they'll fill them with useful paper products; they also have snack baskets stuffed with cocktail napkins, a lined beach basket with a matching towel, and picnic baskets filled with guess what?—picnic utensils. In any case, it takes a lot of bread to buy cache-cache baskets.

GAZEBO / 660 Madison Avenue at 61st Street / Monday through Saturday 9:30 to 5:30 / 832-7077

This is sort of an artsy-craftsy shop, but with a graduate degree. It was one of the prime movers of the basket revival and while it still has woven furniture, pillows and baskets in every shape and form, it has added printed fabric to such a degree that one can momentarily expect the gingham dog to go "Bow-wow-wow" and the calico cat to reply, "Meow."

All the Gazebo's eggs are not in one basket, so the prices range from high to low.

Bath, Bed and Table

If you combine the time you spend between bath, bed and table, you'll find it adds up to a large percentage of each day. This is an excuse—if you need one—for being extravagant with money, thought and energy in making all three as attractive as possible. Since today's life style has extended beyond the narrow confines of fashion's dictate, the N.Y. woman is spending more money, thought and energy on what she will put on her table than on what she is going to put on her back.

Those searching for heavy bedspreads, damask tablecloths and lace-edged finger towels are not apt to find a plethora of them at the shops listed below because we don't use them. But you *will* find sheets and towels, napkins and mats, blanket covers and cocktail napkins for your linen closet, designed by people who once designed things only for clothes closets.

BERGDORF GOODMAN'S LINEN SHOP / 754 Fifth Avenue at 58th Street / Monday through Saturday 10:00 to 6:00, Thursday 10:00 to 8:00 / 753-7300

Bergdorf Goodman's Linen Shop, located in a small alcove on the fourth floor, has all kinds of goodies, some in stock and some to be ordered. Towels, sheets, place mats, tablecloths, blanket covers and the like are all there. The exceptionally nice sales personnel in this department are as pleasant when you buy a cocktail napkin as when a golden Greek special-orders an old-fashioned $3,000 embroidered organdy tablecloth.

*E. BRAUN & COMPANY / 717 Madison Avenue between 63rd
and 64th Streets / Monday through Friday 9:30 to 5:30, Saturday
9:30 to 5:00 / 833–0650*

This small and expensive old-world shop has a surprisingly wide variety of
exquisite linen goods. Many of their linens for bed, bath and table are
still hand-hemmed and can be hand-monogrammed. Chaps who want a
white handkerchief to wave can find fine linen ones here.

*JEAN GALE / 535 Madison Avenue between 54th and 55th Streets
Monday through Friday 9:30 to 6:00, Saturday 10:00 to 5:00
753–2750*

Shower curtains, blanket covers, Swiss embroidered sheets, pillow cases
and comforters are all in stock, and if you can't find what you want, Jean
Gale will custom-make it for you. Also, they carry exquisite, but
expensive, Maderia linens and a full line of children's clothes. Packed
away in every nook and cranny is a full bathroom wardrobe of turkish
towels, washcloths and bath mats in any lovely lush color you might
desire—or if you are a purist, in white.

*LERON / 745 Fifth Avenue between 57th and 58th Streets / Monday
through Friday 9:30 to 6:00, Saturday 9:30 to 5:00 / 753–6700*

Luxury linens with hand-embroidered monograms and French appliquéd
borders for the bath, for the bed and for the table are the trademark of
Leron. They also specialize in off-the-peg or made-to-order nightgowns,
bathrobes and hostess gowns in every fabric from terry cloth to brocade
satin. Divinely beautiful but devilishly expensive.

*LINEN PAVILLION AT SAKS FIFTH AVENUE / East
49th Street between Fifth and Madison Avenues / Monday through
Saturday 10:00 to 6:00, Thursday 10:00 to 8:30 / 753–4000*

The Linen Pavillion at Saks Fifth Avenue used to be called the Carlin
Comfort Shop at Saks and appropriately enough, their specialty was and
still is—comforters. Saks has them in all sizes and shapes, from
down-filled to cashmere throws, and they are all glorious. You'll also find
an array of bath, bed and table goods, and a good selection of pillows
and blankets. Prices range from moderately high to high; but the quality
is consistently good, and if you can wait for a sale, there are bargains to
be had.

PAUL ASSOCIATES / 155 East 55th Street between Lexington and Third Avenues / Monday through Friday 9:00 to 5:00 / 755–1313

Paul Associates has a large selection of bathroom fittings: dolphin faucets, oversized and double medicine chests, attractive door hooks, plain or fancy sinks, mirrors, towel racks, tissue holders, bottles and goblets, and even knobs for the bathroom door. Practically everything comes in a variety of materials, from Lucite to chrome. It's not cheap, but neither is the merchandise.

PLUMMER McCUTCHEON / 145 East 57th Street between Lexington and .Third Avenues / second floor of Hammacher Schlemmer / Monday through Saturday 10:00 to 6:00 / 421–1600

At Plummer McCutcheon you'll find bathroom accessories such as wastebaskets, tissue holders, soap dishes, towel rings and racks, mirrors (including the standing variety), as well as a limited but choice selection of linens for bath, bed and table. In addition, they carry Herend and Spode china and silverware. It's all rich goods.

D. PORTHAULT / 57 East 57th Street between Madison and Park Avenues / Monday through Friday 9:30 to 5:45, Saturday 9:30 to 4:45 / 688–1660

The modern trend of floral bed linen began with D. Porthault. For years the Royal, the Sheik and the Chic have bedded down on Porthault sheets. Their 100% cotton, flowered and geometric prints of percale, batiste or linen are made into sheets, pillow cases, hand towels, blouses, cocktail napkins, place mats, tablecloths, napkins and handkerchiefs. They laminate fabric for picture frames, wastebaskets, tissue boxes, breakfast trays, hangers, eyeglass cases, telephone and address book covers. They also make matching terry cloth for bath towels, hand towels, washcloths, bath and exercise mats, shaving sarongs and bathrobes. Once you've picked a favorite print you can use it for every item listed above. Providing, of course, that expense is no object. If you can't spend $235 on a king-size sheet, you *can* find a picture frame for as little as $10.

PRATESI SHOP / 829 Madison Avenue between 69th and 70th
Streets / Monday through Saturday 10:00 to 6:00 / 288–2315

The Pratesi Shop designs and makes its linens from fine Egyptian cotton
in their Italian factory. If it's natural fabric bedding in plain colors that
suits your fancy, Pratesi is the place to go. But be prepared to pay fancy
prices for plain chic.

SHERLE WAGNER / 60 East 57th Street between Madison and
Park Avenues / Monday through Friday 9:15 to 5:15 / 758–3300

This is probably the best-known bathroom shop in New York and
perhaps in the world. Specialists in custom building and decorating
bathrooms, they can do the job from floor to ceiling and everything in
between. If you have a fantasy bathroom in mind, this is the place to
realize it, whether it be of tubs carved from one block of solid marble;
faucets of silver, pewter, semi-precious gems or 18-carat gold-plate; sinks
of handpainted porcelain in various traditional or contemporary designs.
You dream it; they make it come true. The rude awakening will come
when you get their bill.

Beauty

In New York, women do not have to be born beautiful: the ugliest duckling has a chance of being transformed into a swan with all the beauty care available here. The large beauty salons have a full range of services; the smaller shops we've listed generally specialize in just one phase of beautification.

BEAUTY PRODUCTS AND MAKEUP

BEAUTY CHECKERS AT BENDEL'S / *10 West 57th Street between Fifth and Sixth Avenues / fourth floor / Monday through Friday 10:00 to 3:00 / 247–1100*

Amy Greene, former beauty editor of *Glamour* magazine, created this makeup studio for Bendel's. For $15 an hour (at this writing) a step-by-step lesson is given on how to best apply makeup to get a natural "un-made-up" look. The client is requested to bring her own makeup (although many nonallergenic items are available for purchase), jot down all the hints and to sit and practice until she's perfect. Appointments suggested.

BOYD CHEMISTS / *655 Madison Avenue between 60th and 61st Streets / Monday through Friday 8:00 to 7:00, Saturday 9:00 to 6:00 / closed Saturday July through Labor Day / 838–6558*

A drug store primarily devoted to makeup, Boyd carries, among other things, cosmetics and swansdown puffs and brushes for lips, hair, eyelashes and eyebrows. A place to try new makeup, but be prepared for a slightly hard sell. If you know what you want, you can phone and get speedy delivery.

THE FACE FACTORY / *754 Lexington Avenue between 59th and*
60th Streets / *Monday, Tuesday, Wednesday 9:30 to 6:30,*
Thursday 9:30 to 8:00, Friday 9:30 to 7:00, Saturday 10:30 to 6:00
838–0295

Those who want to try new shades of lipstick, rouge and powder can do
so to their heart's content at the Face Factory. They have endless rows
of rouge and lipstick pots in which to dip your fingers and dab your face.
Once you've found a winning combination, clerks will fill your order
from the house brands. The sampling is gratis; the products are
competitively priced.

ERNO LASZLO INSTITUTE / *10 East 53rd Street between Fifth*
and Madison Avenues / *752–5920*

None of us uses the Laszlo products, but many of our friends won't let
anything else touch their faces. If you're caught up in the Laszlo
mystique, call the Institute (they don't take clients themselves) and they
will refer you to the nearest place where Laszlo products are sold. In
N.Y. they are available at Saks Fifth Avenue and Bergdorf Goodman.

DIANE VON FURSTENBERG / *681 Madison Avenue between*
61st and 62nd Streets / *Monday through Saturday 10:00 to 6:00*
759–2303

Makeup and facials are available at this chic-looking salon. The sales
personnel will advise you of the newest shades, but you must decide
whether they suit you or not, since "new" is not necessarily "becoming."

ELECTROLYSIS

MISS GEMMA LAMA / *608 Fifth Avenue between 48th and 49th*
Streets / *Monday through Friday 8:30 to 5:00* / *757–5159*

Any electrolysis involves a certain amount of discomfort, but it is still the
only way to remove unwanted hairs permanently. Miss Lama is a highly
skilled electrolysist, and her treatments are as painless and fast as any.
Her prices are competitive.

*REBA POMMER / 77 West 55th Street between Fifth and Sixth
Avenues / Monday through Friday 9:30 to 5:30 / by appointment
757–1033*

Reba Pommer is adept at destroying hair roots with both short-wave and
galvanic electric current. She removes unwanted hair from every part of
the body. Her 35 years of experience makes her the electrolysist's
electrolysist. Removing ingrown hairs for gentlemen is one of her skills.
Slightly more expensive than other electrolysists.

EXERCISE

*LOTTE BERK METHOD / 23 East 67th Street between Fifth and
Madison Avenues / fourth floor / Monday through Friday: first
class 8:00, last class 6:30; Saturday: first class 10:00, last class 1:30
288–6613*

You can shape up or slim down at this salon and the exercise won't leave
you with afteraches. The concentration is on ballet movements and
stretching to music, with classes divided according to ability levels. Pay
as you go, $10 per one-hour class. Call for an appointment.

*MISS CRAIG'S EXERCISE PROGRAM / Elizabeth Arden
691 Fifth Avenue between 54th and 55th Streets / Monday
through Friday: private sessions 9:00 to 4:30 / 486–7928*

Marjorie Craig, the author of the best-selling book, *Miss Craig's 21-Day
Shape-Up Program,* teaches her famous body-shaping exercises at
Elizabeth Arden's Fifth Avenue salon. Her program is comprised of
natural movement exercises which trim and shape the entire body and
help to keep it healthy. They can decrease body measurements as much
as an inch in a week's time if you combine the program with diet—or as
much as an inch in two week's time without diet. Because she's so
popular, private lessons with Miss Craig require an appointment, which
usually needs to be made well in advance. Sessions with Miss Craig cost
$15 for one half hour. The other instructors at Arden also use the Craig
exercise method, and give group as well as private lessons. Group lessons
are sold in a series: six people to a class—ten one-hour lessons for $110,
or ten half-hour lessons for $60. Call for an appointment.

RITZ TOWER HEALTH CLUB / 465 Park Avenue at 57th Street / second floor / 421–3580

A small but well-equipped facility for exercise and massage for women. Open to members only but membership can be easily arranged by signing up for five, ten or twenty exercise classes or massages, or a combination of both. A few machines are available, but the emphasis here is on "do it yourself" calisthenics on mats. You may choose group or private exercise classes. (Massages, of course, are private.) To see if you like it, a one-day trial membership is available for $20. Call for an appointment.

EXERCISE CLOTHES

CAPEZIO / 136 East 61st Street between Lexington and Park Avenues Monday through Saturday 10:30 to 5:45 / 758–8833

Leotards and ballet shoes for dancing and exercise, and some pretty shoes for walkers.

FACIALS

GEORGETTE KLINGER / 501 Madison Avenue between 52nd and 53rd Streets / Monday, Tuesday, Thursday, Friday 9:30 to 4:00; Wednesday 9:30 to 3:30, then 5:00 to 7:00; Saturday 9:00 to 3:30 / 838–3200

Facials (for those who like facials) are Klinger's business. Whether your skin has problems or just needs a thorough cleansing, the service here is professional and good. Don't be put off by the assembly-line atmosphere. You need never wait long for an appointment and the prices are reasonable. Eyebrow waxing and dyeing, eyelash dyeing, manicures, pedicures and makeup lessons are also available, as are a multitude of Klinger products—which are pushed. There is a salon for men and boys, too.

HAIR COLORING

NATHAN HAIRCOLOR / 141 East 55th Street between Lexington and Third Avenues / Tuesday through Friday 9:00 to 5:00 / by appointment / 838–5583

One of *the* great hair colorists in New York, Nathan has his own department at Hans and Lars Beauty Salon. He is also an artist at hair-streaking. Expensive but worth it.

THE PRIVATE WORLD OF LESLIE BLANCHARD 19 East 62nd Street between Fifth and Madison Avenues Tuesday through Saturday 9:00 to 5:00, Thursday 12:30 to 8:00 421–4564

The Private World of Leslie Blanchard is where book and magazine editors, movie and stage stars, authors, and suburban housewives go when they want only their hairdresser to know for sure. There *is* a Leslie Blanchard and he has perfected a technique for bringing color to hair with seemingly natural highlights and shadows; this probably explains why Mr. Blanchard is a consultant to Clairol and why women sit on the stairs waiting their turn with him or his special assistant, Gabriella. While the shop does provide its dye customers with manicurists and hairdressers, these services are an accommodation, not a specialty. (Though George *is* a specialist at blow-drying.) It is no more expensive here than at other dye works.

HAIRDRESSERS

ELIZABETH ARDEN / 691 Fifth Avenue between 54th and 55th Streets / Monday through Saturday 9:00 to 5:30 / 486–7900

Travel through the red door into a woman's world that is more than a beauty shop. Treat yourself to a massage, a makeup lesson with Pablo, an exercise class with Marjorie Craig, a hair style by Marc Sinclair—and enjoy a new you. And while you're being beautified, clothes from their second floor ready-to-wear and lingerie department are constantly modeled before your eyes. All services are expensive, and appointments are suggested.

CINANDRE, INC. / 11 East 57th Street between Fifth and Madison Avenues / Monday and Saturday 9:00 to 4:30, Tuesday through Friday 9:00 to 5:30 / 758–4770

A hectic, harried hair salon. The many models (both men and women) who frequent this shop are decidedly *au courant*—as is the decor. The haircuts, too, are up-to-the-minute, but minutes turn into hours while you're waiting your turn, an appointment notwithstanding.

KENNETH / 19 East 54th Street between Fifth and Madison Avenues Monday through Friday 9:00 to 6:00, Wednesday 9:00 to 8:00 752–1800

To many, Kenneth is the Number 1 hair stylist in N.Y., N.Y., and probably the highest priced, too. If it's a haircut or styling you want from Kenneth himself, make an appointment weeks in advance. His other stylists are available and require less notice. If it's a hair treatment you want, ask for Rita; for a set, ask for Jay; for eyebrow arching, ask for Anne; for a facial, ask for Mrs. Hills; for waxing, ask for Sophie. If you want to sit next to celebrities as your hair is cut and set, ask for Mary Farr. She takes care of Jackie and Happy and Mollie. Also, be sure to see the boutique items.

LARRY MATTHEWS / 45 East 55th Street at Madison Avenue Monday through Saturday, open at 7:00 A.M.; appointments made 24 hours a day, if requested; Sunday 9:00 to 5:00 / 246–6100

True, it's mass not class, but it's the only place we know where you can get your hair and nails attended to seven days a week, twenty-four hours a day, by operators who are surprisingly good. And it's very reasonable.

PIERRE MICHEL BEAUTY SALON / 6 West 57th Street between Fifth and Sixth Avenues / Monday, Tuesday, Wednesday 9:00 to 5:00; Thursday, Friday 9:00 to 6:00; Saturday 9:00 to 4:00 by appointment / 753–3995

A model place in the sense that you'll find as many models getting their hair done here as you will on the pages of fashion magazines. It's big and bustling, with lots of good operators to wash, cut and set hair. Be prepared to spend half a day waiting for service, though. Leon, Michael, Suki and Steven Jacobs make it worthwhile. Prices are slightly below the superstar salons, but way above those on Main Street, U.S.A.

RAYMOND AND NASSIR / 18 West 56th Street between Fifth
and Sixth Avenues / Monday through Saturday 9:00 to 6:00;
Thursday 9:00 to 7:00 / 541–8117

There is nothing chi-chi about this place, including the prices. It's
owned and operated by Raymond and Nassir and either of them will
give you a superb "wash and wear" haircut with no fuss or waiting. Side
benefits include an excellent shampoo and very good hair-tinting. Other
services are waxing, manicures, pedicures and facials.

SAKS FIFTH AVENUE BEAUTY SALON / 611 Fifth Avenue
between 49th and 50th Streets / third floor / Monday through
Saturday 10:00 to 6:00; Thursday 10:00 to 7:30 / 486–9460;
486–9466

A beauty shop for shoppers. All the conveniences and services from
hair-coloring (ask for Rosemary), to pedicures, to waxing (ask for Rita),
even to a period hairdo (ask for Margaret). If you have a Saks Fifth
Avenue account, you can charge it. Call for an appointment.

HAIR TREATMENT

DON LEE / 50 West 57th Street between Fifth and Sixth Avenues
Monday through Friday 10:00 to 6:45 / 245–9134

Don Lee is a no-frills hair-care center for both men and women. The
first visit includes a consultation with Mr. Lee to diagnose and
recommend treatment for your specific hair and scalp problem, be it
falling hair, dandruff, dry or oily scalp. Thereafter, once-a-week visits are
suggested (at a cost of $9.25 each). There are no facilities for shampoo
or setting after treatment, so be prepared to rush home or to your
hairdresser.

RITA AT KENNETH'S / 19 East 54th Street between Fifth and
Madison Avenues / by appointment / 752–1800

Rita Prendeville is a hair beautifier. Some ladies go to her once a week
to get their scalps massaged and their hair shampooed, conditioned,
brushed and "swelled" with a high frequency machine. Women with
thinning hair or with hair that lacks body and elasticity, or those who
just want their hair to look naturally shiny and clean, are among the Rita
regulars. People with "good" hair go to Rita, too, but less often. For this
group, she feels that good maintenance requires visits timed to coincide
with the changing seasons.

MANICURE AND PEDICURE

AME / 29 East 61st Street between Madison and Park Avenues
Monday through Friday 9:00 to 6:00; Saturday 9:00 to 5:00
371–1266, 371–1267

If you crave perfect, long, long nails, then plan ahead. Make your
appointment for a manicure in advance (this place is tiny and very busy)
and leave yourself an hour and a half, plus another hour or two until
your polish job has set. The specialty of the house is "paper wrapping"
finger nails to keep them from breaking easily. The resulting manicure
lasts for up to two weeks. The price is $15, including tips. Pedicures can
also be had for $15 (with no paper wrapping).

IRENE / 47 East 77th Street between Madison and Park Avenues
Suite 212 / Monday through Friday 9:00 to 4:00, Saturday 10:00
to 4:00 / 861–7314

This is a one-woman shop and Irene is the woman. She manicures,
pedicures, gives facials, arches and dyes eyebrows and eyelashes and, as if
that weren't enough, also does leg waxing. She knows the paper-wrapping
technique for constructing long beautiful nails and puts polish on like an
artist. Her services cost the same as other luxury beauty salons; but you
don't have to go from operator to operator to get the work done.

WAXING

See Irene (above) and Saks Fifth Avenue (page 28).

Books

Nearly every major book publisher in America calls N.Y., N.Y. home, and we have an abundance of marvelous bookstores that display their wares. Some of the shops are devoted to best sellers and others to special subjects, but no matter what kind of book you are looking for—be it escape reading, a technical tome or a book in a foreign language—you are likely to find it in our town. If you don't believe it, check the Book Dealer's Guide in the Yellow Pages of the N.Y. telephone book, which lists 67 different categories.

ARGOSY BOOKS / 116 East 59th Street between Lexington and Park Avenues / Monday through Saturday 9:00 to 5:00 / 753-4455

An enormous stock of old books, prints and maps can be found here. First editions, medical books and art books are a specialty. Argosy will buy whole libraries, pay cash—and come and get 'em.

BARNES & NOBLE / 105 Fifth Avenue at 18th Street / Monday through Friday 9:45 to 6:45, Saturday 9:45 to 6:00 / 255-8100
600 Fifth Avenue between 48th and 49th Streets / Monday, Tuesday, Wednesday, Friday 9:45 to 6:45, Thursday 9:45 to 8:00, Saturday 9:30 to 6:00 / 765-0590

Barnes & Noble is America's oldest and largest educational bookstore. But in addition to textbooks of every kind, they have a large paperback department and a wide selection of current publications at discount prices. Their discount store is across the street at 128 Fifth Avenue, and the bargains are so terrific that they supply shopping carts to help you collect your loot.

For "I-Love-New York"–ers, who are looking for an unusual keepsake, the new upper Fifth Avenue branch has a New York, New York Boutique, which carries such mementos as 10-inch-long match sticks that depict the Empire State Building!

*BRENTANO'S / 586 Fifth Avenue between 47th and 48th Streets
Monday through Saturday 9:45 to 6:00 / 757–8600*

One of the very best-stocked bookstores in town, it also carries a good
selection of games, museum reproductions and folk art. Their downtown
branch, on Eighth Street, is open on Sunday (see page 132).

*CLASSIC BOOKSHOP / 572 Fifth Avenue between 46th and 47th
Streets / Monday through Friday 9:00 to 8:00; Saturday 9:00 to
6:00 / 586–3990*

A store totally devoted to paperback books.

*DOUBLEDAY / 673 Fifth Avenue at 53rd Street / Monday through
Saturday 9:30 to midnight / 953–4805
724 Fifth Avenue between 56th and 57th Streets / Monday
through Saturday, 9:30 to midnight / 953–4862*

All Doubledays have a wide range of recently published books, a
paperback department and a record section. They are open late and it's
fun to drop in after dinner and find a good book to curl up with.

*MADISON AVENUE BOOKSHOP / 833 Madison Avenue
between 69th and 70th Streets / Monday through Saturday 9:30 to
6:00 / 535–6130*

The neighborhood bookstore of the Upper East Side reading set that
specializes in very expensive books and best sellers. An attractive store
with beautiful displays and gift wrapping, run by nice people.

*RIZZOLI'S INTERNATIONAL PUBLICATIONS, INC.
712 Fifth Avenue between 55th and 56th Streets / Monday
through Saturday 10:00 to midnight / 397–3700*

A bookstore with a truly international flare, Rizzoli's stocks current books
and records in various languages, signed prints, most daily European
newspapers and weekly magazines from around the world. Their
projection room may be rented for private film screenings.

*E. WEYHE, INC. / 794 Lexington Avenue between 61st and 62nd
Streets / Monday through Saturday 9:30 to 5:00 / 838–5466*

Certainly one of the finest art book dealers in the country. Weyhe's also
has a marvelous collection of lithographs and prints for sale. The
knowledgeable salespeople are most helpful.

Boots

Boots are made for walking in winter, wading in water, riding in the rough, rocking at Régine's and sipping in a singles' bar. So if the boot fits, wear them and buy them at the booteries listed below. If you are looking for plain old overshoes, rubbers or toe covers, try the notions counters at department stores or a shoe repair shop.

Children's Boots

INDIAN WALK SHOES / 956 Madison Avenue between 75th and 76th Streets / Monday through Saturday 9:00 to 5:00 / 288–1941

City Boots

DELMAN SHOE SALON / 754 Fifth Avenue between 57th and 58th Streets / Monday through Saturday 10:00 to 6:00; Thursday 10:00 to 8:00 / 759–7600

GUCCI / 699 Fifth Avenue between 54th and 55th Streets / Monday through Saturday 9:30 to 6:00 / closed for lunch 12:30 to 1:30 753–0758; 753–8430

CHARLES JOURDAN / 700 Fifth Avenue at 55th Street / Monday through Saturday 10:00 to 6:00; Thursday 10:00 to 8:00 541–8440; 541–8441

MARIO VALENTINO SHOES / 5 East 57th Street between Fifth and Madison Avenues / Monday through Saturday 10:00 to 6:00 486–0322

Outdoor Sports Boots

HUNTING WORLD INC. / 16 East 53rd Street between Fifth and Madison Avenues / Monday through Saturday 10:00 to 6:00 755-3400

Rain Boots

HENRI BENDEL / 10 West 57th Street between Fifth and Sixth Avenues / Monday through Saturday 10:00 to 5:30 / 247-1110

MISS BERGDORF'S SHOE SALON / 754 Fifth Avenue at 58th Street / Monday through Saturday 10:00 to 6:00, Thursday 10:00 to 8:00 / 753-7300

Riding Boots

See page 198.

Boutiques

Technically, a boutique is "a small shop that carries fashionable clothes and accessories for women." If you add to that definition, "individual service, selection and style," you will have the secret of the success of the many boutiques which have sprung up in N.Y., N.Y. If there is a drawback to what has become the shopping style of the seventies, it is that boutiques, by their very nature, cannot carry the wide range of sizes and colors that a department store does. Countering that is the fact that the individualized selection of clothes makes it less likely that you and a friend will appear at a party in the same dress.

BASHA & / 908 Madison Avenue at 73rd Street / Monday through Saturday 10:00 to 6:00 / 794-8877

When Basha Rudin, a top model, found that she didn't like the clothes being shown on Seventh Avenue, she up and opened her own shop, where she could design and sell the kind of thing she prefers. So for those who like that unconstructed look, this is the place to go for dresses, evening clothes & . . .

EVELYN BYRNES / 480 Park Avenue at 58th Street / Monday through Friday 9:30 to 5:30 / 355-0480

A women's high fashion specialty shop, for those who are more secure wearing top designer clothes and who prefer shopping without the hustle and bustle of a large department store. Not for the young trend-setter or her purse.

COURRÈGES BOUTIQUE / 19 East 57th Street between Fifth and Madison Avenues / Monday through Saturday 9:30 to 6:30, Thursday 9:30 to 7:30 / 755-0300

Vast collections of expensive, but fun, mixable and matchable skirts, pants, shirts and sweaters. One of the original "branders," Courrèges still has his "C" on most items, including those made-to-order. This is not a haven for those who insist on clothes made only of natural fibers.

DANA CÔTE D'AZUR / 750 Madison Avenue at 65th Street
Monday through Saturday 10:30 to 5:30 / 249–1300

French sportswear: a large choice of well-cut shirts, sweaters, pants and skirts to buy separately, or in endlessly enticing combinations. And almost everything is in natural fibers—cotton, silk and wool. If a man happens to be shopping with you, he needn't be bored, for there is also an adjoining boutique for him.

DANSKO / Westbury Hotel / 838A Madison Avenue at 69th Street
Monday through Saturday 10:00 to 6:00 / 879–2105

We go there for simple cotton jackets and jeans with matching tops.

ROBERTA DI CAMERINO / 645 Fifth Avenue at 51st Street
Monday through Saturday 10:00 to 6:00 / 355–7600

Venice's gift to N.Y., N.Y., this ultramodern, opulent shop has luxurious wares to match. Home of the cut-velvet handbag (and wallet, and card case, and luggage), this shop has now expanded to carry trompe-l'oeil patterns in long and short skirts and dresses (and pants and shirts and coats). Only a Doge can afford the prices—and largely for synthetic fabrics at that.

JEANE EDDY, LTD. / 718 Madison Avenue between 63rd and 64th
Streets (up one-half flight of stairs) / Monday through Saturday
10:00 to 5:30 / 371–1950 .

Jeane Eddy has worked her way northward up Fifth Avenue as a buyer for Lord & Taylor, Saks Fifth Avenue and Bonwit Teller to her very own boutique on Madison Avenue. In addition to a sampling of Oscar de la Renta, Diane Von Furstenberg, Donald Brooks and other New York designers, she has her own private-label clothes, belts and jewelry, along with some unique household gadgets and gift items. If she hasn't got what her loyal following wants, she'll get it—and if she can't get it, she'll have it made up. Her sell is soft and her taste impeccable.

SARA FREDERICKS / 508 Park Avenue between 59th and 60th
Streets / Monday through Saturday 9:00 to 5:30 / 759–1255

Another specialty shop for that group that likes name clothes. Its main interest for us is the belts, costume jewelry and the small but choice selection of handbags. Most of these latter items can be viewed right from the Park Avenue window, which can save you a "Thanks, I'm just looking."

FRENCH JEAN SHOP / 227 East 60th Street between Second and
Third Avenues / Monday through Saturday 11:00 to 7:00
486–9888

The fabulous music in this shop makes you want to flip off your clothes
and hustle into every pair of jeans in sight. The levy for these French
jeans is higher than Levi's.

GUCCI SHOPS / 699 Fifth Avenue between 54th and 55th Streets
Monday through Saturday 9:30 to 6:00, closed for lunch 12:30 to
1:30 / 753–0758; 753–8430

Once you've exhausted the Gucci accessories on the ground floor and
crave even more bits and buckles, climb up one flight—but only if there
is still a bulge in your GG wallet. On the mezzanine, you'll find the
apparel to cover the rest of you. Dottore Gucci designs classic shirts,
skirts, dresses, pants and coats in suedes, silks and wools—and they're all
beautifully made.

HALSTON / 33 East 68th Street / entrance on Madison Avenue
Monday through Friday 10:30 to 5:45, Saturday noon to 5:00
794–0888

Here is Halston's own world and its capital is Ultrasuede. In this, his
own boutique, you'll find all of Halston's numbered collections: III, his
raincoats; IV, his lounge wear; V, his less expensive sportswear. On the
first floor are innumerable cashmere sweaters, silk blouses, skirts, pants,
scarves, hats and a few men's clothes. Up the winding staircase is a vast
array of long and short dresses, pants outfits, the Halston fragrance,
handbags, luggage and Elsa Peretti jewelry. It all adds up to elegant,
expensive simplicity. Around the corner (on 68th Street) is Halston
Couture. Even more elegant, expensive and simple, it can be entered by
appointment only.

T. JONES / 1050 Third Avenue at 62nd Street / Monday through
Saturday 9:45 to 6:00 / 838–5990
11 East 57th Street between Fifth and Madison Avenues
Monday through Saturday 10:00 to 5:45 / 758–9660

T. Jones translates the great American sportswear look into carefully
tailored, meticulously-made separates for the Country Club look. There
are shirts, sweaters, dresses, coats, pants and accessories, and they all
match. The tariff is reasonable, yet the emphasis here is on quality of
workmanship—and it shows. There's a wide selection of small sizes with
truly correct proportions.

JULIE ARTISANS GALLERY / 687 Madison Avenue at 62nd Street / Monday through Saturday 11:00 to 6:00 / 688–2345

Julie lives and sells her precept, "Fashion is an art form." From her list of artists she commissions one-of-a-kind wearables. Her clothes are so far into the realm of fantasy that if they aren't on your back, they can be hung on the wall. Art is costly, and so are her treasures—but browsing is free, and some of her delightful pillows, stuffed dolls and body jewelry are well worth seeing.

KNITY / 134 1/2 East 62nd Street between Lexington and Third Avenues / Monday through Thursday 11:00 to 7:00, Friday and Saturday 11:00 to 6:00 / 832–2152

Knity sells custom-made knitted dresses, sweaters and suits at prices lower than those usually charged for custom-made items. They have certain basic styles which they will adapt to your choice of shape, color and even pattern. A few floor samples can be bought "off the peg"; for custom-made, allow 2 to 3 weeks.

LADY CONTINENTAL / 836 Madison Avenue at 69th Street Monday through Saturday 10:00 to 6:00 / 988–0110

Known mainly for its European-made copies of Chanel shoes, Lady C also has a small boutique with handsome shirts, sweaters, skirts and well-cut pants—mostly imported from Europe at well-up prices.

TED LAPIDUS PARIS / 666 Fifth Avenue at 53rd Street / Monday through Saturday 10:00 to 5:45, Thursday 10:00 to 8:30 582–5911
1010 Third Avenue at 60th Street / Monday, Thursday 10:00 to 9:00, Tuesday, Wednesday, Friday, Saturday 10:00 to 7:00 751–7251

If you're looking for a superbly tailored pure silk shirt in an unusual shade, you probably will find it at Lapidus, along with beautifully coordinated accessories like, for example, a belt, hat, sweater and skirt that match perfectly. The look is very *haute sportif Français* and so are the prices. Men's clothes are in the same genre, but beware of gift-giving if your man's preference has been J. Press and Brooks Brothers till now.

*MARTHA, INC. / 475 Park Avenue at 58th Street / Monday through
    Saturday 9:30 to 6:00 / 753–1511*

New York's top designers love this shop—it always has a large selection
of their latest designs. And, important to the purchaser, they're kept in
mint condition. At Martha's you will also find European favorites such as
Valentino, Mila Schöen and Andre Laug. Not for those with anemic
clothing budgets or weak sales resistance.

*NADELIA / 645 Madison Avenue between 59th and 60th Streets
    Monday through Saturday 10:00 to 6:00 / 832–9381*

Nadelia has pants, blouses and skirts in sizes 4 to 14, all imported from
France and Italy. Depending upon the season, the selection ranges from
cotton to crepe de chine. For summer she expands her collection to
include dresses, blazers and caftans. Summer prices start at $50, and as
the temperature goes down, the starting prices go up (to $70).

*NEW YORK JAX / 7 West 57th Street between Fifth and Sixth
    Avenues / Monday through Saturday 10:00 to 5:00 / 753–5866*

The emphasis here is on matching separates for the trim and slim. Their
pants are true finds for ladies with nothing to hide. The N.Y. Jax, like
the California original, specializes in checked ginghams and calicos which
are made into everything from lined slacks to petticoated dresses, skirts,
jackets. Their clothes also come in wools, velvets and the like. If they
haven't an outfit in your size, they'll special order; and if you don't like
the patterns in stock, you may choose colors and fabrics from their
voluminous swatch books.

*SCALERA KNITWEAR / 794 Madison Avenue between 67th and
    68th Streets / Monday through Saturday 10:00 to 6:00 / 988–3344*

The large selection of hard-to-find silk knits, cotton knits and 100% wool
shirts and sweaters found in the rear of this shop is hard to beat, and the
styles are classic. The polyester separates in the front of the shop are
easy to ignore. The prices are fair.

*ALICE SCHWEITZER / 739 Madison Avenue between 64th and
65th Streets / Monday through Friday 10:00 to 6:00, Saturday
11:00 to 5:00 / 861–3350*

Expensive ensembles—pants suits, skirt suits, dresses and blouses—are a
specialty. They are mostly imports from France and mostly small sizes.
All, however, are of good quality and made with much attention paid to
detail. A small selection, but a good one.

*ST. LAURENT RIVE GAUCHE BOUTIQUE FEMME
855 Madison Avenue between 70th and 71st Streets / Monday
through Saturday 10:00 to 5:45 / 988–3821*

This is the fashion "groupies'" place for this year's look, no matter
which country, culture and century is the source of Yves's current
inspiration. It's his authentic boutique line transplanted directly from
Paris. Any copies made on Seventh Avenue need not apply. This shop
concentrates on a narrow range of blouses, sweaters, skirts, pants, dresses
and coats, plus accessories—all beautifully made. The price for this kind
of chic is high.

*SWEATER CENTER LTD. / 697 Madison Avenue between 62nd
and 63rd Streets / Monday through Friday 10:00 to 6:00, Saturday
10:00 to 5:00 / 838–1835*

If you have a passion for sweaters, this is the place for you. Sweaters in
just about every hue of the rainbow can be found in wool, cashmere or
blends—all in a wide range of styles and sizes. The sales staff is friendly,
eager to help and willing to unfold and refold and unfold and . . .
Medium prices are an extra bonus.

*SWEELO / 689 Madison Avenue at 62nd Street / Monday through
Saturday 10:00 to 6:00 / 688–2310*

Sweelo has style for those who know their own style. Fairly inexpensive
prices mark its soft silk blouses, cotton knits and silk-looking caftans. It
has a contemporary jewelry collection that is not to be taken seriously,
but is fun. The selection here is constantly changing, so there is always a
mélange of unusual European and young American boutique clothes.

TAPEMEASURE / 799 Madison Avenue between 67th and 68th Streets / Monday through Friday 10:00 to 6:00, Saturday 10:00 to 5:45 / 249–9220
1031 Third Avenue at 61st Street / Monday and Thursday 10:30 to 8:30, Tuesday, Wednesday, Friday 10:30 to 6:30, Saturday 10:30 to 6:15 / 758–2050

Ready for the young and young-at-heart are jeans, T-shirts, dresses, suits with skirts and pants, and coats. Great for all ages is the Tapemeasure made-to-order department. There are models in various sizes which can be modified to your measurements and duplicated in the fabric of your choice. The service is rapid and reasonable for made-to-order clothing.

ANN TAYLOR / 15 East 57th Street between Fifth and Madison Avenues / Monday, Tuesday, Wednesday, Friday 10:00 to 6:45, Thursday 10:00 to 7:45, Saturday 10:00 to 5:45 / 753–7203

The windows of this once staid shop give a pretty good picture of what is selling inside. There are lots of reasonably priced separates and dresses for daytime and after-six, all in the newest and trendiest styles of the underfed and under-forty set. An occasional prowl through, to check the latest arrivals and other customers, is great fun and highly informative as to the current state of fashion.

VALENTINO / Fifth Avenue between 53rd and 54th Streets / Monday through Saturday 10:00 to 6:00 / 421–7550

This famous Italian designer opened his new shop in 1975. Here, amidst a myriad of mirrors, is a mélange of beautiful sweaters, shirts, dresses, coats and pants—all those things that make up *haute couture* sportswear. Only for those who have an open-ended clothes budget. The men's department in this shop rivals the ladies' in space and price.

VALESKA NEW YORK / 820 Lexington Avenue at 63rd Street Monday and Thursday 10:00 to 8:00, Tuesday, Wednesday, Friday 10:00 to 6:30, Saturday 10:00 to 6:00 / 752–6895

The offerings run the gamut from French blue jeans to jackets, dresses, nightgowns, robes, bikinis, sweaters, hats—all mostly for the young-young. The lady who runs this shop is a regular visitor to the French *prêt à porter* (ready-to-wear) shows and therefore her merchandise reflects the latest Paris scene, but happily not at Paris prices.

*VENEZIANO BOUTIQUE / 819 Madison Avenue between 68th
and 69th Streets / Monday through Friday 10:00 to 6:00, Saturday
11:00 to 6:00 / 988–0211*

This boutique is a favorite of *Women's Wear Daily,* so it attracts people
who don't mind having publicized what they've purchased, right down to
the number and color of favorite dresses, sweaters, pants, shirts, bags and
whatever. Veneziano has skinny pants for skinny derrières, and skimpy
shirts for the under-endowed. All its clothes are "with it," stylishly priced
and imported from Italy. But if you wear anything larger than a size 10
—it's *"ciao,* baby."

*WOMEN'S HABERDASHER / 680 Madison Avenue at 62nd
Street / Monday through Saturday 10:00 to 6:00 / 838–7140
995 Madison Avenue at 77th Street / Monday through Saturday
10:00 to 6:00 / 988–0865*

There are only a few styles to choose from at this well-named emporium,
but it fills a definite need for the hard-to-fit customer who is also
well-heeled. You can have a classic suit, coat, dress, or pants
made-to-order in a very short time. The workmanship is excellent. The
fabrics may change from one year to the next, but the styles go on and
on forever.

*WRANGLER WRANCH / 1074 Third Avenue between 63rd and
64th Streets / Monday, Tuesday, Wednesday, Friday 10:00 to 7:00,
Thursday and Saturday 10:00 to 8:00 / 371–0838*

European visitors in the know make a beeline for Wrangler Wranch for
the presents most welcomed back home. There's everything in denim for
anyone who has anywhere from a 26-inch to a 42-inch waist, including,
of course, the great American obligatory wardrobe item, Wrangler jeans.
The big thing at the Wranch is jackets, jeans and shirts—if you want to
go West-ern you can get it all together here. And cheaply, too.

*YVES ST. TROPEZ / 4 West 57th Street between Fifth and Sixth
Avenues / Monday through Saturday 9:30 to 6:30 / 765–5790
251 East 60th Street between Second and Third Avenues
Monday through Saturday 10:00 to 6:30 / 759–3784*

Ici on parle français! The real knockouts here are the imported silk and
cashmere shirts and sweaters with beautiful, misty, handpainted designs.
The collection of blouses, pants suits, skirts and coats is handsome, but
good only for those built like a French mademoiselle. *Très cher.*

Buttons

*TENDER BUTTONS / 143 East 62nd Street between Lexington and
Third Avenues / Monday through Friday 11:00 to 6:00, Saturday
11:00 to 5:30 / closed Saturday during July and August
758–7004*

Button, button, who's got the button? Tender Buttons, that's who!
They've got thousands and thousands of samples of Victorian, French,
English, cloisonne, enameled, handpainted, jet and flower fasteners used
in days gone by. In other words, just about any type of button can be
found here, including an enormous selection of blazer buttons—old and
new. The rarer the button, the rarer the price.

Candles

BEESWAX CANDLES

*BLOOMINGDALE'S CANDLE SHOP / Separate entrance on
East 59th Street between Lexington and Third Avenues / Monday
and Thursday 9:45 to 9:00; Tuesday, Wednesday, Friday, Saturday
9:45 to 6:00 / 355-5900*

*RENAISSANCE ART GALLERY / 185 East 80th Street between
Lexington and Third Avenues / Monday, Tuesday, Thursday,
Friday 11:00 to 5:00 / closed during summer / 988-3736*

RIGAUD CANDLES

The landslide winner as today's replacement for potpourri or incense is the
French Rigaud candle. Rigauds come in two scents—cypress and cypher—
and in three sizes—small, medium and large. (Our particular favorite is the
large cypress.) Regardless of what scent or size you choose, it'll be like
burning money, for they're expensive. Yet other scented candles don't seem
to hold a candle to Rigaud's fresh aroma.

Rigaud candles can be bought at the four "B's": Bendel's, Bergdorf's,
Bloomingdale's and Bonwit's.

VOTIVE CANDLES

*AZUMA / 666 Lexington Avenue between 55th and 56th Streets
Monday through Saturday 10:00 to 9:00 / 752-0599*

*LAMSTON'S / 773 Lexington Avenue at 61st Street / Monday and
Thursday 8:00 A.M. to 8:00 P.M., Tuesday and Wednesday 8:00 to
6:15, Friday and Saturday 8:00 to 6:45 / 751-0885*

Candy

Popular candy bars can be found at newsstands and grocery counters, but listed below are the fancier sweets for sweethearts and very sweet tooths.

GODIVA CHOCOLATIER INC. / 701 Fifth Avenue between 54th and 55th Streets / Monday through Saturday 10:00 to 6:00 593–2845

Godiva is known for its sweet, expensive and elaborately boxed candy.

KRON CHOCOLATIER / 764 Madison Avenue between 65th and 66th Streets / second floor / Tuesday through Saturday 10:00 to 6:00 / 288–9259

This unique chocolatier makes his product right on the premises. For a novel and delicious greeting card, you can order one of the hand-decorated specials with a message of your choice. A visual and gustatory treat. Pear-shaped chocolate shells for home-filling and candy-covered strawberries are two other goodies at this shop. For do-it-yourselfers, they also have classes in the art of chocolate-making.

PLUMBRIDGE / 33 East 61st Street between Madison and Park Avenues / Monday through Friday 9:30 to 5:00, Saturday 11:00 to 4:30 / 371–0608

There are highly original and edible gifts here in beautiful, often reusable packages—for example, the white Chinese spice jar filled with spiced nuts. Our favorite, the "Cabinet," is a small chest with five pull-out drawers filled to order with spiced nuts, candied fruit, mocha-covered nuts and chocolates. About four pounds of deliciousness for $28. (Larger sizes, with larger prices, are available too.)

SIMON PURE / 49 East 57th Street between Madison and Park Avenues / Monday through Saturday 9:00 to 5:45 / 832–3238

This is the best place to buy low-calorie hard candies, which come close to satisfying that craving for sweets.

Charity Shops

There are three different kinds of establishments that fall under the general category of "charity shops." To the first you donate old clothes, furniture, etc., for resale; the charity receives the proceeds, which you may claim as a tax deduction. The second kind offers new merchandise, often made by the needy and sold by volunteers, with the profits shared by the creators and the charity. Finally, there are the shops in hospitals and museums, where highly unusual new merchandise (museums offer reproductions of pieces from their own collections) is sold for the benefit of the institution. In addition to the museum shops specifically listed below, the shops at the Guggenheim and the Whitney are well worth a visit.

AMERICAN MUSEUM OF NATURAL HISTORY / Central Park West at 79th Street / Monday through Saturday 10:00 to 4:45, Sunday and holidays 11:00 to 5:00 / 873–1300

There are three shops at this museum: one for adults and the other two for children. The adult shop features jewelry from nearly every country including China, but with special emphasis on American Indian and Mexican artifacts. The Museum's shops also carry pottery, planters, microscopes, glassware with etchings of endangered species, reproductions of totem poles, clothing from India, Morocco and Africa—and dinosaur kits for young paleontologists.

ELDER CRAFTSMEN SHOP / 850 Lexington Avenue between 64th and 65th Streets / Monday through Friday 10:00 to 5:30, Saturday 10:00 to 4:00 / 535–8030

This shop features the finely made handicrafts of the elderly, with a fine selection of baby clothes, needlepoint, pillows, Christmas stockings, afghans and other things found nowhere else. If you have a special gift in mind, the Elder Craftsmen Shop can often find the right person to make it for you. This is a nonprofit organization and the prices are within reason.

LIGHTHOUSE / 111 East 59th Street between Lexington and Park Avenues / Monday through Friday 10:00 to 5:00 / 355-2200

All year round the Lighthouse shop is a place to find handicrafts made by the blind.

Once a year, wealthy women donate their clothes, furniture, paintings, or any object in good condition, for one major sale here to raise money to help the blind.

METROPOLITAN MUSEUM OF ART / Fifth Avenue at 82nd Street / Tuesday 10:00 to 8:30, Wednesday through Saturday 10:00 to 4:30, Sunday 11:00 to 4:30 / 879-5500

The Metropolitan pioneered the method of helping to support itself by selling reproductions of objects from its collection. It's a perfect place to find presents of silverware, china, glassware, costume or real gold and silver jewelry. If it's art books you're after, they've got a fine selection. Prices are low; museum members get a discount.

MUSEUM OF THE CITY OF NEW YORK / Fifth Avenue at 103rd Street / Tuesday through Friday 10:00 to 4:30, Saturday 10:00 to 4:45, Sunday 1:00 to 4:45 / 534-1672

The shop in this museum caters primarily to children and is appropriately stocked and priced. The merchandise consists mainly of reproductions of toys, miniature bottles, doll-house-scale furniture, and other items that are historically related to New York City. In addition they have silver wares and a few fine books.

MUSEUM OF MODERN ART / 11 West 53rd Street between Fifth and Sixth Avenues / Monday, Tuesday, Friday, Saturday, Sunday 11:00 to 5:45; Thursday 11:00 to 8:45 / 956-7070

This museum shop is best known for its 20th-century art books and Christmas cards. The Modern's approach to museum reproductions has been to commission contemporary artists to design small sculptures, prints, etc., to sell for the benefit of the museum. Members are given a discount on these items and in addition receive the comprehensive Christmas catalogue.

NEW YORK EXCHANGE FOR WOMEN'S WORK
541 Madison Avenue between 54th and 55th Streets / Monday through Friday 9:30 to 5:00, Saturday 10:00 to 4:00 / 753-2330

The Exchange was founded as a nonprofit organization to help sell crafts created by women. It now incorporates on the ground floor an inexpensive, no-nonsense restaurant which is good for a quick stop while shopping. The second-floor gourmet department purveys wonderful pâté, chicken salad and casseroles to take home. The homemade jams, jellies, preserves, pastries and a fine plum pudding in season are our favorites. The gift shop has antiques and beautiful handiwork for all ages, crocheted booties and bed jackets and handknitted dolls and sweaters.

Children's World

There is more for children in N.Y., N.Y. than any other place in the world. There is culture, clothing, food, fun, eye-boggling sights and shows to see. There are trips to take, sports to see and do, animals to ogle and even to feed, and toys of every size, shape and price to buy and take home. In other words, there's no better place to broaden a child's horizons than where the buildings reach higher than an elephant's eye.

CLOTHES

BERGDORF GOODMAN / 754 Fifth Avenue at 58th Street
Monday through Saturday 10:00 to 6:00, Thursday 10:00 to 8:00
753-7300

This boys' and girls' clothes department is really the place for grandmothers with big hearts and purses to match. Though the stock is small, what is available is exquisite. For girls over 12, there's another shop on the same floor, called "Bigi."

*BLOOMINGDALE'S / Lexington Avenue between 59th and 60th
Streets / Monday and Thursday 9:45 to 9:00, Tuesday,
Wednesday, Friday, Saturday 9:45 to 6:00 / 355–5900*

The children's department here is more like a three-ring clothes circus
for the "Health-Tex" set, that is, from newborns to teen-agers. The
selection is enormous, moderately priced and ranges in style from very
simple to very "mod."

*BROOKS BROTHERS / 346 Madison Avenue at 44th Street
Monday through Saturday 9:15 to 6:00 / 682–8800*

The boy in the gray flannel suit probably bought it at Brooks Brothers.
For generations, mothers have taken their sons to Brooks for their first
grown-up get-up. Here the young gentlemen from size 8 on up to size 20
can be outfitted from top to bottom, from inside to out, in the
button-down Brooks Brothers look. Suits start at $90 and sports jackets at
$45. Other merchandise is comparably priced.

*CERUTTI, INC. / 807 Madison Avenue between 67th and 68th
Streets / Monday through Saturday 9:30 to 5:45 / 737–7540*

Children's wear from Cerutti, Inc. is the chicest and the most expensive
in town. They have their own exclusive designs, plus a lovely
made-to-order department, as well as such name designers as Florence
Eiseman. The size-range is from infants' to 14.

*GLAD RAGS / 1007 Madison Avenue between 77th and 78th Streets
Monday through Saturday 9:00 to 6:00 / 988–1880*

This is a specialty shop for shirts, jeans and jackets. The casual and
outdoor wear here is mostly washable, durable and expensive.

*JEAN GALE / 535 Madison Avenue between 54th and 55th Streets
Monday through Friday 9:30 to 6:00, Saturday 10:00 to 5:00
753–2750*

Jean Gale offers a small selection of elegant children's clothes geared to
the toddler-tricycle trade. Top tariffs, too.

*PAT-RICK / 930 Madison Avenue between 73rd and 74th Streets
Monday through Saturday 9:45 to 5:45 / 288–1444*

This is the store to go to find matching brother and sister outfits. These cleverly designed clothes, with handpainted or embroidered motifs, are mostly ready-to-wear at reasonable prices.

*SAKS FIFTH AVENUE / 611 Fifth Avenue between 49th and 50th
Streets / Monday through Saturday 10:00 to 6:00, Thursday 10:00
to 8:30 / 753–4000*

Saks' children's department has a fine selection of clothes for boys and girls. Some are simple, some are fancy, some are designed by Suzie of Saks, some are expensive—all are fashionable. Actually, Saks can take care of boys' and girls' clothing needs from the cradle on up.

*WENDY'S / 1046 Madison Avenue between 79th and 80th Streets
Tuesday through Saturday 11:00 to 6:00 / 861–9230*

Wendy carries shirts, handpainted T-shirts, jeans, jackets, overalls and coats for the playground group. Most of the clothes here are practical for rough-and-ready wear.

EATS

*AUTOPUB / 767 Fifth Avenue between 58th and 59th Streets
Monday through Friday 11:45 to 10:00, Saturday and Sunday
11:30 to 3:00 / 832–3232*

The booths resemble auto bodies of olden days and many youngsters we know invariably select this slightly dark, slightly crowded spot as their favorite Fifth Avenue lunch stop. The fare is mostly for children and features—what else? Hamburgers! Prices are moderate but not cheap.

*BASKIN-ROBBINS / 1010 Third Avenue at 60th Street
Monday through Sunday 11:00 to 11:00 / 688–8458; 838–9816
925 Lexington Avenue at 68th Street / Monday through Sunday
10:00 to 10:00 / 650–1982*

Baskin-Robbins is nearly always crowded because it is one of N.Y.'s favorite ice creameries. Lots of flavors are sold in cones, sundaes, sodas and in bulk. You can eat on the premises, if you're prepared to stand, but primarily this is a take-out ice cream parlor with one-scoop cones costing 45¢.

*BUN & BURGER / 645 Madison Avenue at 60th Street / Monday
    through Friday 11:00 to 9:00, Saturday 11:00 to 7:00 / 826–0688*

We've never known a child who didn't like the Bun & Burger
hamburgers—for breakfast, lunch, dinner or in-between. The counter and
take-out service at this restaurant expedites the care and feeding of
children.

*McDONALD'S / 966 Third Avenue between 58th and 59th Streets
    Monday through Friday 7:00 to 1:00 A.M., Saturday 8:00 to 2:00
    A.M., Sunday 8:00 to midnight / 753–5360*

Our neighborhood, like almost every neighborhood across the U.S., has
its own McDonald's, serving its "Big Macs" and all the usual trimmings.

*PALEY PARK / East 53rd Street between Fifth and Madison Avenues
    Monday through Saturday May through October 8:00 to 7:00,
    November through April 8:00 to 6:00 / closed January*

This tiny oasis has a waterfall in the background, trees planted here and
there, benches, chairs and tables placed conveniently about, and the best
hot dogs in town. The vending booth is to the right of the entrance,
designed to be inconspicuous in order not to mar the beauty of the park.
N.Y. buffs love it, even though it replaced their old favorite haunt, the
Stork Club.

*SERENDIPITY 3 / 225 East 60th Street between Second and Third
    Avenues / Sunday through Friday 11:30 to midnight, Saturday
    11:30 to 2:00 A.M. / 838–3531*

This is the home of the 12-inch hot dog (with or without chili), the
gooiest sundae around, bigger-than-life sodas complete with three straws
and plenty of whipped cream. Perfect fare for the greedy, and at the
same time a dieter can keep pace with a low-calorie bean sprout, or other
vegetarian, delight. In order to get to the restaurant you must wade
through the boutique with its penny candy and novel "wears."

SERVICES

CENTRAL PARK KINDERGARTEN AND DAY CAMP
1 West 89th Street at Central Park West / Monday through Friday 8:30 to 5:30 / 724-8488

Children from two and a half to eight years old can enjoy music and learn crafts here in small play groups. Hot lunches are served. When there is a vacancy, the Central Park Kindergarten will accept children for a minimum of one week. The monthly rate is $160. If transportation is needed, add $45.

MOLE BARBER SHOP / 1021 Lexington Avenue at 73rd Street
Monday through Saturday 8:00 to 6:00 / 535-8461

This is a haircutting place that's been around for a long time. Generations of children have felt safe getting their locks shorn here. The barbers are many in number and all competent, as well as being understanding about children and their hair. Appointments recommended, but if shearing is a pressing priority, this shop is accommodating. Prices are competitive.

SIGHTS TO SEE

AMERICAN MUSEUM OF NATURAL HISTORY / Central
Park West at 79th Street / 873-4225: recorded announcement gives details of activities and hours.

This museum is devoted to the natural history of the world and has to be seen to be believed. It's a must for children, though adults will love it, too. It will take more than one trip to see it all, but no matter how short your visit is, be sure to see the dinosaur gallery and the Hall of Minerals and Gems.

*BRONX ZOO & CHILDREN'S ZOO / Fordham Road between
180th and 190th Streets / Monday through Saturday 10:00 to 5:00,
Sunday and holidays 10:00 to 5:30 / 220–5100; recorded
announcements on traveling instructions and hours: 933–1759*

This beautiful park is devoted to a large collection of animals and birds
gathered from all over the world, living in natural settings and habitats.
There are electric carts to transport you between the different areas and
an aerial tramway that provides a spectacular overall view of the zoo, but
even more fun for children are the special areas where they can play
with baby animals and, for a fee, ride on a horse or a camel. It's a day
well spent, if the weather is good.

*CENTRAL PARK ZOO / Fifth Avenue at 64th Street / daily 11:00
to 5:00 / 472–1003*

Central Park Zoo has a small collection of animals and birds, plus a
special area where children may walk among, and pet, young farm
creatures. Often to be found is a variety of unscheduled open-air
magicians and musicians; ethnic food carts and balloons are always
around. Seal-feeding time at 2:30 is the highlight of spring and summer
days.

THE CLOISTERS

See page 126.

*HAYDEN PLANETARIUM / Central Park West at 81st Street
Monday through Friday 2:00 and 3:30, Saturday hourly from 11:00
to 5:00, Sunday 1:00 to 5:00 / 873–8828*

Hayden Planetarium's show explains the starry skies and solar system to
the fascination of young and old alike. The action takes place overhead
as you sit in comfort in the darkened theater. Admission price is $2.35
for adults; $1.35 for children seventeen years and under, and for students
with I.D. cards.

*MUSEUM OF THE CITY OF NEW YORK / Fifth Avenue at
103rd Street / Tuesday through Saturday 10:00 to 5:00, Sunday
1:00 to 5:00 / 534–1672*

This is New York City's own museum devoted to collecting clothes,
silver, jewelry, furniture, paintings, theater artifacts—anything and
everything pertinent to our City. Both parents and children will enjoy
the display of doll houses and the toys of past and present generations, as
well as the large collection of fire engines. The whole family can sit and
view with delight the N.Y. panoramic film show, in which the history of
N.Y. unfolds with real props from the museum collections. And, it's all
for free.

*NEW YORK BOTANICAL GARDEN / located behind the
Bronx Zoo, see page 52 / daily 10:00 to 7:00
220–8700*

The N.Y. Botanical Garden's beautiful old greenhouse holds one of the
world's largest collections of rare flora. Surrounding outdoor gardens are a
treat in spring. Admission is free to pedestrians.

Guided Tours

*BURLINGTON HOUSE "THE MILL" / 1345 Avenue of the
Americas between 54th and 55th Streets / Tuesday through
Saturday 10:00 to 7:00 / 333–5000*

This free tour of a replica of a Burlington textile mill is designed to
demonstrate how fabric is made. The tour starts with the basic raw fiber
that step-by-step is spun, then woven, then dyed and processed—and
finally emerges as a giant bolt of cloth. Educational for children;
fascinating for adults.

CIRCLE LINE SIGHTSEEING / boats leave from Pier 83 at the foot of West 43rd Street / call for schedule: 269–5755

The Circle Line tour is a lovely way, on a hot summer's day, to prove that Manhattan really is an island. Here's the best view of the Statue of Liberty and the Battery, the World Trade Center and Wall Street, the Brooklyn Bridge, the United Nations complex, the Chrysler and Empire State Buildings, the high-rise luxury buildings of the East Side. The West Side offers the George Washington Bridge and, further down, ocean liners and cruise ships docked at the piers. A running commentary, lots of sitting and standing room fore and aft all make a pleasant three hours afloat. This costs $5.00 for adults and $2.50 for children under twelve years old. There are reasonably priced snacks and beverages. Also inquire about the ferry boat excursions to the Statue of Liberty.

EMPIRE STATE BUILDING / 350 Fifth Avenue between 33th and 34rd Streets / Monday through Sunday 9:30 to midnight 736–3100

The Empire State may no longer be the highest building in town (the World Trade Center is) but she's still the grande dame of skyscrapers and the hub of mid-Manhattan. Ears pop as you travel up in the elevators, and eyes pop when you see the spectacular view this landmark offers. Cost: $1.75 for adults and 85¢ for children.

ROCKEFELLER CENTER / 50 West 50th Street, between Fifth and Sixth Avenues / guided tours: Monday through Sunday 9:30 to 5:30 / 489–2947

There are two tours available at Rockefeller Center: the first takes you through the buildings, explaining the history of the Center and its art work. There is also a visit backstage at Radio City Music Hall, and a final stop at the top of the observation tower. The one-hour walking tours leave from 50 West 50th Street. Tours start at $2.25 for adults, $1.40 for children.

UNITED NATIONS / First Avenue between 42nd and 48th Streets /
tours leave every 15 minutes, daily 9 to 4:45

A tour of the headquarters of the United Nations features an explanation of its history, structure and programs, and visits to the major halls, including the General Assembly and the Security Council (when they're not in use). Weekdays it is possible to eat in the delegates' dining room. Reservations are not required, although it is advisable to call in advance.

Tour rates are $2 for adults, $1.50 for college and high school students, and $1 for elementary school children. Children under 5 are not admitted.

Television Tours

Many national television shows emanate from New York, and audiences are permitted to view some of them. Call the major broadcasting companies listed below and inquire what they have to show.

WABC (Channel 7) 1330 Avenue of the Americas at 54th Street
581-7777

WCBS (Channel 2) 51 West 52nd Street at Sixth Avenue
975-4321

WNBC (Channel 4) 30 Rockefeller Plaza between Fifth and Sixth
Avenues / 247-8300

WNET (Channel 13) 356 West 58th Street between Eighth and
Ninth Avenues / 262-4200

WNEW (Channel 5) 205 East 67th Street between Second and
Third Avenues / 585-1000

WOR (Channel 9) 1440 Broadway at 40th Street / 764-6683

WPIX (Channel 11) 220 East 42nd Street at Second Avenue
949-1100

SKATING

LE PETIT / 213 West 58th Street between Broadway and Seventh Avenue 9:30 to 9:00 / Private lessons Monday through Sunday 581–4960

This is a skating studio, not a regular-size rink. Practice time is available by appointment.

ROCKEFELLER CENTER / Fifth Avenue at 50th Street / lower plaza / call for schedule of daily sessions: 757–5730

Outdoor ice-skating in a beautiful setting from October through April. Admission is $4 per session; $3 for children under 12 years old. Instructions and skate rentals available.

SKY RINK / 450 West 33rd Street between Ninth and Tenth Avenues call for schedule of sessions and for prices: 695–6555

Indoor skating, all year round.

WOLLMAN RINK / Central Park, 59th Street entrance between Fifth and Sixth Avenues, opposite St. Moritz Hotel / or use 64th Street entrance from Fifth Avenue, which closes at dusk / call for schedule of daily sessions: 593–8229

Wollman Rink is a large outdoor skating rink in the woodlands of Central Park. It is open from November through mid-March. Skates can be rented except for figure skating sessions. Weekday prices: $1.25 for adults; 25¢ for children under 14. Saturday rates: $1.75 for adults; 50¢ for children under 14.

TOYS

RAPPAPORT TOY BAZAAR / 1381 Third Avenue between 78th and 79th Streets / Monday through Saturday 10:00 to 6:00, Thursday 10:00 to 8:00 / 879–3383

A worldful of toys from around the world. Often the less expensive playthings that aren't available at F. A. O. Schwarz can be found at Rappaport's. Their selection is vast, which makes it easy for children to pick out what they want Santa to bring them, and therefore "Santa" likes it, too.

F. A. O. SCHWARZ / 745 Fifth Avenue at 59th Street / Monday through Saturday 10:00 to 6:00, Thursday 10:00 to 8:00 644–9400

F. A. O. Schwarz is one of the largest, and certainly one of the most famous, toy stores in the world. Merchandise ranges from tops and kites to sporting equipment, board games, dolls, doll houses, costumes, lead soldiers, stuffed animals, and more. In addition, they feature a huge selection of electric trains, and even miniaturized automobiles that children can sit in, turn the power on and drive. Don't look here for bargains.

China

Fine chinaware and pottery are available in hundreds of different patterns in our town. A good jumping-off place is the department stores. At one or another you'll find the contemporary patterns of Lenox, Spode, Wedgwood, Minton, Royal Worcester, Ginori, Royal Crown Derby, Royal Limoges and copies of others, such as Meissen's Blue Onion pattern. For further options, try Tiffany and Cartier (who also carry fine china in patterns exclusive to them) and/or the shops we've listed below. If it's the rare old porcelain you want, check Antique Dealers (see page 5).

Inexpensive

AZUMA / 666 Lexington Avenue between 55th and 56th Streets Monday through Saturday 10:00 to 6:30 / 752–0599

Limited selection sold in sets or separately.

THE POTTERY BARN / 117 East 59th Street between Lexington and Park Avenues / Monday and Thursday 10:00 to 8:30, Tuesday, Wednesday, Friday 10:00 to 6:30, Saturday 10:00 to 6:00, Sunday noon to 5:00 / 838–7130

Stackable pottery, cups, dishes, etc.

More Expensive

CACHE-CACHE / 758 Madison Avenue between 55th and 56th
    Streets / Monday through Friday 10:00 to 5:30, Saturday 11:00 to
    5:00 / 744–6886; 747–7060

Small selection of own designs. Also breakfast sets.

CARDEL, LTD. / 615 Madison Avenue between 58th and 59th
    Streets / Monday through Friday 9:45 to 5:45, Saturday 9:45 to
    5:30 / 753–8880

Traditional patterns, plus Lalique glassware.

CERALENE CHINA AT BACCARAT, INC. / 55 East 57th
    Street between Madison and Park Avenues / second floor
    Monday through Saturday 9:30 to 5:30 / 826–4100

Fine Limoge place settings.

MICHAEL FINA / 580 Fifth Avenue at 47th Street / second floor
    Monday through Friday 9:00 to 5:30 / 757–2530

Good traditional and modern place settings at discounted prices.

GINORI FIFTH AVENUE / 711 Fifth Avenue between 55th and
    56th Streets / Monday through Saturday 10:00 to 6:00, Sunday
    noon to 5:00 / 752–8790

Ginori carries its own Italian china, as well as others.

GEORG JENSEN, INC. / 601 Madison Avenue between 57th
    and 58th Streets / Monday through Saturday 10:00 to 6:00,
    Thursday 10:00 to 7:00 / 935–2800

Scandinavian china.

PLUMMER McCUTCHEON / 145 East 57th Street between
    Lexington and Third Avenues / second floor of Hammacher
    Schlemmer / Monday through Saturday 10:00 to 6:00 / 421–1600

Herend and other traditional china patterns, as well as a good selection
of large serving plates and platters.

ROYAL COPENHAGEN PORCELAIN / 573 *Madison Avenue between 56th and 57th Streets / Monday through Saturday 9:30 to 5:30 / 759–6457*

Danish china, including Flora Danica.

SCULLY & SCULLY / 506 *Park Avenue between 59th and 60th Streets / Monday through Friday 9:30 to 5:30, Saturday 10:00 to 5:00 / 755–2590*

A small selection of fine china, including Herend.

CAROLE STUPELL, LTD. / 61 *East 57th Street between Madison and Park Avenues / Monday through Saturday 9:30 to 6:00 / 260–3100*

Mostly modern, highly styled tableware.

Cleaners

See page 72.

Coats

Nowhere in the world will you find a larger selection of coats than in N.Y., N.Y.. They are available in all lengths, weights, fabrics and styles. Whether you are after a cloth, fur, goose down, a reversed lambskin or a raincoat, try the large department stores first—every one of them has several extensive sections for outdoor wear. Traditionally, Election Day and Columbus Day are coat sale days in our town, and bargains abound at this time.

Very few people (except experts in the field) can judge the quality of furs. We have listed below, however, the names of furriers with whom we have done business over the years and have found to have good quality, style—and markups. Many we know buy furs wholesale; we do not nor do we recommend it.

BERGDORF GOODMAN / 754 Fifth Avenue at 58th Street
 Monday through Saturday 10:00 to 6:00, Thursday 10:00 to 8:00
 753-7300

The fur department at Bergdorf's has a large selection of coats, from sable to skunk. The quality is excellent and the designs are all in good taste—continuing in the footsteps of the late, great Emeric Partos. There's a recent addition of furs by Fendi, the Italian designer. Fendi's boutique and the fur department are only steps from one another in distance and in price. For the less expensive, more trendy furs, the Miss Bergdorf fur department rates a stop.

MAXIMILIAN FUR COMPANY / 20 West 57th Street between
 Fifth and Sixth Avenues / Monday through Friday 9:30 to 5:30
 247-1388

Maximilian has a reputation for being the most elegant, innovative and expensive furrier in New York. It's deserved, and Madame Potok can take the bows for it.

REISS & FABRIZZIO, INC. / 724 Fifth Avenue between 56th and 57th Streets / Monday through Friday 9:30 to 5:00, Saturday by appointment / 245–0322

This furrier specializes in mink, sable and broadtail—all of fine quality and simple designs. Beautiful furs are expensive commodities, so it pays to shop. This is one of our stops.

RITTER BROS.– BEN THYLAN FURS / 32 East 57th Street between Madison and Park Avenues / fourth floor / Monday through Friday 9:00 to 5:00, Saturday 9:00 to 12:30 / 753–7700

Several companies, formerly having done business in the low-rent fur district of the West 30's, joined forces in this large showroom in the higher-rent district. Guess what happened to their prices? But there's a large selection of stylish, quality furs available. A specialty of the house is a fur lining that fits into several different outer shells. This means you can have a fur-lined silk raincoat, all-weather coat, tweed coat or even a fur-lined fur coat, merely by changing the outer shell.

SAKS FIFTH AVENUE / 611 Fifth Avenue between 49th and 50th Streets / Monday through Saturday 10:00 to 6:00, Thursday 10:00 to 8:30 / 753–4000

The well-known French furrier, Revillion Frères, took over the Saks Fifth Avenue fur department many years ago and has been selling N.Y. women their sables, minks, broadtails, foxes and the like ever since. There's a lot to choose from, and if what you want isn't in one Saks, they'll call it in from a branch store. No bargains, except at sale time.

Cooking Utensils

See page 115.

Couture Clothes

We all love our Seventh Avenue and the vast majority of our clothes come from its designers. But there may be an occasion when you want a dress to be yours and yours alone, and for that reason we add these couturiers.

CEZ ET BEZ / 135 East 65th Street at Lexington Avenue / Monday through Friday 9:00 to 4:30 / by appointment / 288–1789

Though Cez & Bez have their own models, they will make clothes from photographs in magazines, copy your old favorites, and even make clothes that you design. You may select fabric from the many samples on hand, or supply your own.

CHEZ NINON / 487 Park Avenue between 58th and 59th Streets third floor / Monday through Saturday 9:00 to 5:00 / appointments suggested / 753–6821

Chez Ninon is the only shop we know that copies Paris models line-for-line. Prices start at $2,000.

HALSTON / 33 East 68th Street at Madison Avenue / Monday through Friday / by appointment / 794–0888

Halston has a couture division which you enter at 33 East 68th Street. Here the clothes are different from, but similar to, his ready-to-wear. It's elegant made-to-order and we love it. Although these clothes are not made with the same fine stitch as the Parisian couture, they don't carry the same fine price tags either.

ARNOLD SCASSI, INC. / 681 Fifth Avenue between 53rd and 54th Streets / by appointment / 755–5105

Made-to-order clothes of haute style and haute price. Scassi produces two collections a year.

Decorators

All good decorators bring their own style to every job. If that style goes hand-in-hand with your taste—you've found the perfect decorator for *you*. Decorators know antique and modern furniture, and prices; they know fabrics, lighting, floor coverings, wall hangings and where to find whatever you are looking for—that's why we use them. Altman's, Bloomingdale's, Lord & Taylor's and W. J. Sloane's all have resident decorators. There is no charge for this service, but all goods must be purchased through their stores at retail prices.

The decorators we have listed below base their fees on retail prices also; in other words, they buy wholesale and charge you retail. All are by appointment only.

BRASWELL ASSOCIATES / 235 *East 57th Street* / 421–0373

CRONIN-STEMPLER DESIGN, CO. / 225 *East 57th Street* 688–3389

CHARLES R. DEAR, INC. / 440 *East 57th Street* / 759–8597

DENNING & FOURCADE / 125 *East 73th Street* / 759–1969

MARK HAMPTON / 46 *East 65th Street* / 879–9006

MELANIE KAHANE / 251 *East 61st Street* / 755–2421

M.A.C. II / 121 *East 81st Street* / 249–4466

ELLEN L. McCLUSKEY ASSOCIATES / 654 *Madison Avenue* / 838–6850

McMILLEN / *148 East 55th Street* / *755–3600*

PARISH-HADLEY / *22 East 69th Street* / *249–2920*

RICHARD L. RIDGE INTERIOR DESIGN / *903 Park Avenue* / *472–0608*

Department Stores

You'll find, as a rule, that as you work your way uptown from 34th to 58th Streets, the department stores gradually change from general merchandise marts to ladies' specialty shops. For example, Altman's devotes as much, if not more, space to home furnishings as it does to women's apparel. With Lord & Taylor, at 39th Street, the balance begins to shift to women's wear, although the home is still important. By the time you reach the 50's, Saks and three of the B's (Bendel's, Bergdorf's, and Bonwit's) concentrate almost totally on milady. The fourth B, Bloomingdale's, of course, is a world of its own and is a law unto itself. Merchandise necessarily overlaps, but still, each department store has a few specialties that make it unique.

B. ALTMAN & COMPANY / *Fifth Avenue between 34th and 35th Streets* / *Monday through Saturday 10:00 to 6:00, Thursday 10:00 to 8:00* / *689–7000*

Altman's is the last of the old carriage trade stores. It is big and cavernous and maintains a very wide range of quality goods. Though it is off our beaten path, the really helpful and polite salespeople make shopping here a pleasure. There is a good antique department; an interesting selection of house furnishings, dishes, glasses, kitchenware and notions; an excellent stock of sheets and some sheeting by the yard; clothing departments for men and women of all ages and sizes; a gourmet food department; and a luncheon restaurant called the Charleston Gardens. Altman's is also known for its Waterford crystal and other Irish imports.

HENRI BENDEL / 10 West 57th Street between Fifth and Sixth
Avenues / Monday through Saturday 10:00 to 5:30 / 247–1110

Bendel's is small and very chic, just like the woman who shops there. Perfectly edited clothes and accessories are to be found, but beware if you're bigger than a size 10 or conservative in your tastes. One of the special attractions is the street floor of boutiques where you can find, among other things, unique accessories, gifts, stationary and E.A.T.S. Other finds are clothes by Holly's Harp, Sonia Rykiel and Mary McFadden; the bridal department; Savvy (for young and mod tastes); the lingerie and at-home departments. Note: The Christmas catalogue is a great source of ideas for inexpensive presents with a flair.

BERGDORF GOODMAN / 754 Fifth Avenue at 58th Street
Monday through Saturday 10:00 to 6:00, Thursday 10:00 to 8:00
753–7300

This store has spread from what was once the Vanderbilt mansion to cover the entire west side of Fifth Avenue from 58th to 57th Streets. It has traditionally catered to a clientele that feels at home in lush surroundings, but the custom-made copies of French originals have disappeared, along with the horse-drawn carriages that once deposited ladies at the 58th Street door. Today, that lady's daughter arrives by taxi and heads for the Halstons, the Givenchy boutique and the superb fur department. The fine lingerie area at Bergdorf's is also a favorite, as is the Titkiner sportswear fresh from the south of France. Other nooks and crannies that she, and we, especially appreciate are the men's department and barber shop, Jo Hughes—Bergdorf's very special personal shopper— the linen shop, Bigi's Bite for the fastest lunch in town, the children's department and the only hosiery counter we know of that allows try-ons.

*BLOOMINGDALE'S / Lexington Avenue between 59th and 60th
Streets / Monday and Thursday 9:45 to 9:00, Tuesday,
Wednesday, Friday, Saturday 9:45 to 6:00 / 355-5900*

Bloomingdale's is a state of mind. It has given birth to a whole
generation that feels that "Bloomie's" is the center of its shopping
universe. The Bloomingdale addict is of any age, either sex, any
pocketbook and any station in life—even the Queen of England stopped
traffic to see it. Bloomingdale's merchandise is as varied as the customer.
Our favorite spots are the gourmet food department, including the bread
counter; the teeming cosmetic area where a makeup demonstration is
usually in progress; the men's section with very fashionable haberdashery;
the handbags and hats, accessories and blouses, right out of the pages of
Harpers' Bazaar and *Vogue;* the comprehensive housewares department;
the bedding section's enormous selection of basics and the furniture floor
with its changing display of model rooms. Congratulations are in order
for the Bloomingdale buyers—more often than not, they have stocked
the latest gadget we thought we alone had discovered abroad.

*BONWIT TELLER / 721 Fifth Avenue at 56th Street / Monday
through Saturday 10:00 to 6:00, Thursday 10:00 to 8:00
355-6800*

Bonwit Teller is typical of the uptown department store in that it is
basically devoted to ladies' apparel. Our favorite haunts here are the
Hermès boutique; the Turnbull and Asser shirt counters in the men's
department and in the women's blouse department; the Missoni
boutique for slinky Italian knits; Orsini's lunch spot on the second floor
and Mr. Jennings' old-fashioned ice-cream parlor on the ninth; the S'fari
Room devoted to up-and-coming designers from all over the globe; the
shoe salon with its own Charles Jourdan boutique; and last but not least,
the gift and housewares floor, with a What's Cooking Kitchen. The
Kitchen is a real honest-to-goodness cooking department, where culinary
techniques are demonstrated.

GIMBELS / Broadway at 33rd Street / Monday and Thursday 9:45 to 8:30, Tuesday, Wednesday, Friday 9:45 to 7:00, Saturday 9:45 to 6:00, Sunday and holidays noon to 5:00 / 564-3300
125 East 86th Street at Lexington Avenue / Monday, Thursday, Friday 10:00 to 9:00; Tuesday, Wednesday, Saturday 10:00 to 7:00, Sunday and holidays noon to 5:00 / 348-2300

Gimbels at 33rd Street is the store to watch for sales. To many, their strength is their housewares, from flatware and dinnerware for the table, to sheets and comforters for the bed. Excellent buys can nearly always be had at Gimbels, but the department that pleases us most is the one devoted to stamps and rare coins, where there's a lot for the collector to see and savor.

The uptown branch's stock does not compare with that of the 33rd Street emporium.

LORD & TAYLOR / 424 Fifth Avenue at 38th Street / Monday through Saturday 10:00 to 6:00, Thursday 10:00 to 8:00 / to order merchandise: 391-3300; for all other business: 391-3344

Lord & Taylor, one of New York's landmark stores, has been around for a hundred and fifty years. It is solid in the sense that if you (and enough others to make it worthwhile) find something you like, the store continues to stock it. Lord & Taylor also keeps up with the times in clothes, home furnishings for inside and out, decorating fabrics by the yard, and with a resident staff of interior decorators to help you "do" a chair, a room or an entire house. L. & T. is probably best known for the wide selection of classic sportswear, dresses and shoes. It's just had its face lifted (wouldn't you at that age?) but happily the soup bar and Bird Cage restaurant for salads and sandwiches remain the same.

MACY'S / Broadway at 34th Street / Monday, Thursday, Friday 9:45 to 8:30, Tuesday, Wednesday, Saturday, 9:45 to 6:45, Sunday and holidays noon to 5:00 / 971-6000

Everything about Macy's is larger than life—including its Thanksgiving Day Parade. The store itself has to be seen—it has everything: quality goods, furs and jewels and antiques, wearing apparel for you, yours and your house from top to bottom. Something new is always happening at Macy's. This year it's their basement, renamed "The Cellar," and among the new things present "down under" is a branch of savvy New Yorkers' beloved P.J. Clarke's, which serves the best hamburgers and chili in town; plus gourmet shops with super fresh produce, mod furniture room displays and "hip" clothes—all at Macy's prices, which usually means cheaper.

SAKS FIFTH AVENUE / 611 Fifth Avenue between 49th and 50th Streets / Monday through Saturday 10:00 to 6:00, Thursday 10:00 to 8:30 / 753-4000

If it's clothes you are looking for—men's clothes, boys' clothes, women's clothes, girls' clothes, babies' clothes, expensive clothes, less expensive clothes, inner clothes, outer clothes, winter clothes, summer clothes, imported clothes, domestic clothes, designer clothes, sports clothes, formal clothes—try Saks first. It has the strongest fashion departments of any of the Fifth Avenue stores. The fifth floor is the home of a host of well-known designers including Adolfo, Bill Blass, Donald Brooks, Oscar de la Renta, Mollie Parnis, Kaspar and last, but not least, *Charlotte Ford!* In addition to clothes, Saks excels in handbags, shoes, Vuitton luggage, and linens. You'll also find well-stocked counters selling gloves, scarves, sunglasses, and even travel accessories. If you think we like it—you're right.

PRICE-LESS STORES

ALEXANDER'S / 731 Lexington Avenue between 58th and 59th Streets / Monday through Saturday 10:00 to 9:00, Sunday noon to 5:30 / 593-0880

Alexander's is basically a discount store with fashionable trappings. We use it for very specific items, such as gloves, stockings and costume jewelry. If you're not in the market for luxury goods, and enjoy ferreting out your "bargain of the week," Alexander's could be for you.

KORVETTE'S / 1293 Broadway at 34th Street / Monday, Thursday, Friday 9:30 to 9:00, Tuesday, Wednesday, Saturday 9:30 to 7:00, Sunday 11:00 to 6:00 / 564-7700
    140 East 45th Street between Lexington and Third Avenues Monday through Friday 8:30 to 6:30, Saturday 9:30 to 6:00 986-9400
    575 Fifth Avenue at 47th Street / Monday and Thursday 9:30 to 9:00, Tuesday, Wednesday, Friday 9:30 to 7:00, Sunday 11:00 to 6:00 / 867-7000

Korvette's is one of those places that sells name brands at reduced rates along with the cheaper lines of many manufacturers. It carries clothes, small and large electrical appliances for the kitchen, and TVs, radios, tape decks, etc. It also has good buys in best-selling books, but don't go there if you don't have the patience to wait, or if you need the helpful suggestions of a knowledgeable clerk. Also good for nonprescription drugs (see page 71).

*LEXINGTON MART / 686 Lexington Avenue between 56th and
57th Streets / Monday through Friday 9:00 to 5:30, Saturday 10:00
to 2:30 / 755–1154*

The Mart's motto is the old standard, "We will not be undersold." They
have small appliances, televisions, radios and cameras—all discounted at
differing rates, up to 30% less than the going prices elsewhere. Anything
they don't have on the premises they usually can get with a little notice.

*OHRBACH'S / 5 West 34th Street between Fifth and Sixth Avenues
Monday and Thursday 10:00 to 8:30, Tuesday, Wednesday, Friday
10:00 to 6:45, Saturday 10:00 to 6:00, Sunday and holidays noon
to 5:00 / 695–4000*

Ohrbach's is a "cut-rate" department store with high fashion at low
prices. Twice a year they show their own exact copies of European *haute
couture* clothes. There's always a scramble for tickets for this event.

Designer Clothes

Since N.Y., N.Y. is the fashion capitol of the world, it is little
wonder that nearly every well-known American designer is
headquartered here. Despite this proximity, "We can't get it
for you wholesale." We can, however, tell you which shops
carry which designers. (If we have omitted your favorites, just
look them up in the New York telephone book, then call and
ask, "What store carries your clothes?") Being where it's all
at is just one of the joys of living in N.Y., N.Y.

ADOLFO   Saks Fifth Avenue

*GEOFFREY BEENE   Altman's, Bergdorf Goodman, Lord &
Taylor, Martha, Saks Fifth Avenue*

BILL BLASS Bergdorf Goodman, Bonwit Teller, Evelyn Byrnes, Lord & Taylor, Martha, Saks Fifth Avenue

DONALD BROOKS Bloomingdale's, Bonwit Teller, Lord & Taylor, Saks Fifth Avenue

ALBERT CAPRARO Altman's, Bloomingdale's, Bonwit Teller, Lord & Taylor, Saks Fifth Avenue

CHLOÉ Saks Fifth Avenue

OSCAR DE LA RENTA Altman's, Bergdorf Goodman, Bonwit Teller, Evelyn Byrnes, Sara Fredericks, Lord & Taylor, Saks Fifth Avenue

CHRISTIAN DIOR Saks Fifth Avenue

CHARLOTTE FORD Bergdorf Goodman, Bonwit Teller, Evelyn Byrnes, Martha, Saks Fifth Avenue

HALSTON Bergdorf Goodman, Bloomingdale's, Martha, Halston's own shop at 813 Madison Avenue at 68th Street

KASPER Elizabeth Arden, Bergdorf Goodman, Bloomingdale's, Bonwit Teller, Sara Fredericks, Lord & Taylor, Saks Fifth Avenue

KIMBERLY Bergdorf Goodman, Bloomingdale's, Bonwit Teller, Evelyn Byrnes, Sara Fredericks, Lord & Taylor, Saks Fifth Avenue

MOLLIE PARNIS Elizabeth Arden, Bergdorf Goodman, Bloomingdale's, Bonwit Teller, Evelyn Byrnes, Sara Fredericks, Lord & Taylor, Martha, Saks Fifth Avenue

DOMINIC ROMPOLLO Bergdorf Goodman, Evelyn Byrnes, Sara Fredericks, Lord & Taylor, Martha, Saks Fifth Avenue

PAULINE TRIGÈRE Bergdorf Goodman, Bonwit Teller, Evelyn Byrnes, Sara Fredericks, Lord & Taylor, Saks Fifth Avenue

DIANE VON FURSTENBERG Altman's, Bergdorf Goodman, Bloomingdale's, Bonwit Teller, Lord & Taylor, Saks Fifth Avenue

Drug Stores

BOYD CHEMISTS / 655 Madison Avenue between 60th and 61st Streets / Monday through Friday 8:00 to 7:00, Saturday 9:00 to 6:00 / closed Saturday July through Labor Day / 838–6558

A working pharmacy, this shop also specializes in European makeup products (see page 22) and has a great selection of hairbrushes.

CASWELL-MASSEY CO., LTD. / Lexington Avenue at 48th Street / Monday through Saturday 10:00 to 5:45 / 755–2254

A large assortment of soaps, house scents and sundries awaits you at this chemist and perfumer. Caswell-Massey has been in business in America since 1752, and the products they offer reflect the good old days and ways.

EDWARD'S DRUG STORE / 225 East 57th Street between Second and Third Avenues / Monday through Saturday 8:30 to 9:00, Sunday 10:00 to 5:00 / 753–2830; prescription department: 753–2885

Open seven days a week, it has a prescription department and a full range of medicine and sundries.

KAUFMAN PHARMACY / Lexington Avenue at 50th Street / never closes / 755–2266

Most drug stores close at 6:00, so at odd hours Kaufman's is the emergency stop for most midtowners.

KORVETTE'S / 140 East 45th Street between Lexington and Third Avenues / Monday through Friday 8:30 to 6:30, Saturday 9:30 to 6:00 / 986–9400
    575 Fifth Avenue at 47th Street / Monday and Thursday 9:30 to 9:00, Tuesday, Wednesday, Friday 9:30 to 7:00, Sundays and holidays 11:00 to 6:00 / 867–7000

If you know your milligrams, this is the place to buy vitamins or nonprescription pills at low prices.

WILLIAM RADOFF / 806 Lexington Avenue at 62nd Street
    Monday through Friday 9:00 to 7:00, Saturday 10:00 to 6:00
    838–2500

This old-fashioned chemist is a fun place to visit when searching for nonsense gifts and stocking-fillers. Its serious business is prescriptions and hospital supplies, and hairbrushes that our hairdressers go there to buy.

C. & R. TIMMERMAN / 799 Lexington Avenue between 61st and
    62nd Streets / Monday through Saturday 9:00 to 7:00 / 838–5580

A brightly lit, nicely stocked drug store that will deliver in the area, with a smile.

Dry Cleaners

Hand laundries and nonassembly-line dry cleaners are increasingly hard to find, and yet for special clothes (men's prized shirts and ladies' precious dresses) nothing else will do. Other cleaners suffice for everyday clothes. We have some cleaners who treat each garment with individual attention and loving care and charge a pretty penny; and others are fine for less expensive clothes.

B. J. DENIHAN / 505 East 75th Street between York Avenue and
    East River Drive / Monday through Friday 8:30 to 5:30, Saturday
    8:30 to noon / 535–7900

One of the oldest and most expensive cleaners in the City. Some of us think it's the best, and others refrain from comment.

ELAINE HOLDER / 867 Madison Avenue near 72nd Street
Monday through Friday 9:00 to 6:00 / 288–3940

One of the better dry cleaners, they can be trusted with your most
precious dress. Mrs. Holder will try to accommodate you about time, but
generally likes a week if a garment is badly spotted. Knits come home
not only clean but properly blocked and sized. Expensive, but excellent.

IRIS CLEANERS AND DYERS / 131 East 56th Street between
Lexington and Park Avenues / Monday through Friday 7:30 to
5:00, Saturday 8:00 to 12:00 / 753–3028

A good small neighborhood cleaner that will pickup and deliver, with
24-hour service if you request it, at relatively reasonable rates. They're
good for men's shirts and even make the effort to return stray cuff links
and studs.

LEATHER CRAFT PROCESS OF AMERICA / 54 West
56th Street between Fifth and Sixth Avenues / Monday through
Friday 9:00 to 5:00, Saturday 9:00 to 1:00 / 586–3737

They will clean suede and leather gloves, handbags and clothing. Be
prepared to sign a waiver releasing the store from responsibility, should
the leather goods not come back as good as new. Snip off buttons
yourself, as they are liable to be ruined in the cleaning process.

MME. BLANCHEVOYE / 75 East 130th Street between Madison
and Park Avenues / Monday through Friday 7:00 to 3:30, pickup
and delivery, mornings only / 722–7260

Mme. does the finest job of hand-laundering in New York, especially on
linens.

MME. DEE ET MME. YVONNE FRENCH CLEANERS
1382 Third Avenue between 78th and 79th Streets / Monday
through Friday 8:00 to 6:30, Saturday 8:00 to 5:00 / 737–4238

Superb cleaning, if you do not need instant service. Expensive, but they
treat your garments with T.L.C.

Emergency Services

Life, unfortunately, is not without emergencies, large and small. We have gathered a list of telephone numbers of emergency services available in our town. Though nearly every hospital has an emergency clinic, we have included a few that are in our neighborhood.

ALCOHOLICS ANONYMOUS / 468 Park Avenue South
686–1100

AMERICAN EXPRESS COMPANY / American Express Plaza between Broad and Water Streets / 797–3131; credit card division customer service: 677–5500

AUTOMOBILE CLUB OF NEW YORK / 28 East 78th Street at Madison Avenue / 586–1166; emergency road service: 695–8311; travel service & highway weather conditions: 594–0700

CRESCENT SERVICE STATION (gasoline station) / First Avenue and 62nd Street / never closes / TE 8–9755

DENTAL EMERGENCY SERVICE OF THE FIRST DISTRICT DENTAL SOCIETY / 759–9609

DRUG ADDICTION CENTER / The Hot Line: 787–7900

FIRE   Dial "O" for operator

KAUFMAN PHARMACY / Lexington at 50th Street / never closes PL 5–2266

KEEFE AND KEEFE AMBULANCE SERVICE / 429 East 75th Street / never closes / 988–8800

PAUL MOR (diesel gas) / First Avenue and 117th Street / Monday through Saturday 6:00 A.M. to 7:00 P.M. / 289–9842

PASSPORT OFFICE / 630 Fifth Avenue at 50th Street / 541–7700

POLICE / 911

Hospital Clinics

LENOX HILL HOSPITAL / 100 East 77th Street at Park Avenue 794–4567

MANHATTAN EYE, EAR, AND THROAT HOSPITAL 210 East 64th Street between Second and Third Avenues 838–9200

NEW YORK HOSPITAL OF THE CORNELL MEDICAL CENTER (PRIVATE) / 528 East 70th Street at York Avenue / 472–5050

Employment Agencies

(for domestic help)

The Classified Ad sections of the local newspapers are devoted largely to business and commercial job opportunities; therefore, when searching for household help, most New Yorkers rely on employment agencies. These establishments are required by law to check the references of any job seekers they recommend to their clients. Both the employer and the employee are charged a fee of roughly 15% of the first month's salary for live-in help, 13% for those who live out and 10% for temporary accommodators. You can interview job applicants at your own home or at the agency.

FINNISH EMPLOYMENT AGENCY / 954 Madison Avenue at 75th Street / Monday through Friday 9:00 to 5:00 / 288–6562

HEDLUND / 699 Madison Avenue between 62nd and 63rd Streets Monday through Friday 9:00 to 4:00 / 355–3244

A. E. JOHNSON / 954 Madison Avenue at 75th Street / Monday through Thursday 9:00 to 4:30, Friday 9:00 to 4:00 / 734–6719

MADAME S. JACQUIN AGENCY / 29 East 61st Street between Madison and Park Avenues / Monday through Friday 9:00 to 1:00 593–2985

Eyeglasses

Eyeglasses are generally a necessity, but today they are also a fashion item. The variety of eyeglass frames available in New York is enormous, so if you can't find what you are looking for in one of the stores listed below—perhaps you should have your eyes re-examined. All these places do a good fitting job and are very obliging about readjusting loose frames, no matter where they were purchased.

LUGENE OPTICIANS. / 38 East 57th Street between Madison and Park Avenues / Monday, Tuesday, Wednesday, Friday 9:00 to 5:30, Saturday 9:00 to 5:00 / 486–7500

E.B. MEYROWITZ, INC. / main store: 520 Fifth Avenue between 43rd and 44th Streets / Monday through Friday 8:30 to 5:45, Saturday 9:00 to 4:00 / 682–3880
    555 Madison Avenue between 55th and 56th Streets / Monday through Friday 9:00 to 5:30, Saturday 9:00 to 4:00 / 753–7536
    839 Madison Avenue between 69th and 70th Streets / Monday through Friday 9:00 to 5:30, Saturday 9:00 to 4:00 / 628–9202

A. R. TRAPP / 488 Madison Avenue between 51st and 52nd Streets Monday through Friday 9:00 to 6:00, Saturday 10:00 to 4:00 752–6890

Fireplace Equipment

Department stores that feature furniture among their wares usually carry a few fireplace utensils, though fireplace specialty shops are a better source for mantels, unique andirons and other accessories. The cognoscenti, when all else fails, head downtown, where a great variety of brass and copper fittings can be found in the many shops clustered around Orchard and Green Streets on the Lower East Side. The fireplace specialty shops listed below have kept our home fires glowing for years.

EDWIN JACKSON / 306 East 61st Street at Second Avenue
Monday through Friday 9:00 to 5:00 / 759–8210

Edwin Jackson, a specialist in fireplace equipment, caters to both wholesale and retail trade. This establishment sells period and reproduction fireplace seats, fenders, andirons, screens and tools. They have modern and antique mantels of wood and marble, either carved or pristine. Service and installation is part of their charming, old-world approach.

WILLIAM H. JACKSON / 3 East 47th Street at Fifth Avenue
Monday through Friday 9:00 to 4:30 / 753–9400

William Jackson has a very large selection of quality fireplace utensils, as well as antique and modern mantels.

Five-and-Ten-Cent Stores

LAMSTON'S / 466 Lexington Avenue at 45th Street / Monday through Friday 8:00 to 6:00, Saturday 9:30 to 5:30 / 684–3923
    477 Madison Avenue at 51st Street / Monday through Friday 8:00 to 6:00 / 688–0232
    773 Lexington Avenue at 61st Street / Monday and Thursday 8:00 A.M. to 8:00 P.M., Tuesday and Wednesday 8:00 to 6:15, Friday and Saturday 8:00 to 6:45 / 751–0885

WOOLWORTH'S / 976 Third Avenue at 59th Street / Monday and Thursday 9:30 to 8:45, Tuesday, Wednesday, Friday, Saturday 9:30 to 6:30 / 755–8634
    441 Fifth Avenue at 39th Street / Monday through Saturday 8:30 to 5:50 / 685–3431

Fixers

Accident-prone or not, everyone breaks something sometime. Unfortunately, stores cannot be as service-oriented as they once were—so specialists have arisen to fix everything; the trick is to find them. Those we've unearthed are listed below.

BELTS

JIM'S SHOE REPAIRING AND HAT RENOVATING CO. / 50 East 59th Street between Madison and Park Avenues Monday through Friday 8:00 to 6:00, Saturday 8:00 to 4:00 355–8259

Like all good shoe repair shops, Jim also fixes belts.

CANEWORK

YORK END ANTIQUES / *1278 First Avenue between 68th and 69th Streets* / *Monday through Friday 10:00 to 6:00, Saturday 10:00 to 6:30* / *722–9584*

Canework is done on these premises. York End Antiques stocks pre-woven cane in five sizes: small, regular, medium, large and very large. They can match or totally recane a chair (back and seat), table top, bench, headboard or whatever. Their charges are computed at the rate of one dollar an inch. For example, a chair seat measuring 14 by 16 inches would cost $16. There is a small additional charge for pickup and delivery.

DOLLS

NEW YORK DOLL HOSPITAL / *787 Lexington Avenue between 61st and 62nd Streets* / *second floor* / *Monday through Saturday 9:30 to 6:00* / *838–7527*

If you have a doll or toy animal made of rag, porcelain, papier-mâché, wood, or vinyl and plastic compounds that needs a doctor, the New York Doll Hospital is the place to go. For over fifty years they have been operating without having lost a patient, and furthermore, they don't bury their mistakes. They will even perform hair transplants with synthetic or real hair blends. This is where battery-run self-destructive dolls come for reconstruction and where antique dolls come for restoration. Antique dolls are bought, sold, rented and appraised. Doll clothes are in stock or couture models can be made to order.

FRENCH INVISIBLE MENDING

ELAINE HOLDER / *867 Madison Avenue near 72nd Street Monday through Friday 9:00 to 6:00* / *288–3940*

French invisible mending is a dying art in America, but in New York you can still get it done. Mrs. Holder applies this classic technique to woolens, silks (depending upon the nub of the fabric) and even some polyesters. On some materials mending can't be invisible, but even Mrs. Holder's visible mending is well done.

GLASSWARE

HESS REPAIRS / 200 Park Avenue South at 17th Street / Monday
through Friday 10:30 to 4:00, Saturday 11:00 to 3:00 / 260–2255

Specialty of the house—those impossible-to-find blue liners for silver salt
cellars, which makes Hess worth the trip downtown. They have saved
many a cut 'twixt the cup and the lip by grinding down the edges of
chipped crystal goblets.

SANDOR HOWARD / 791 Lexington Avenue between 61st and
62nd Streets / Monday through Friday 10:30 to 4:00 / 355–9827

Repairs to chipped glass and porcelain are the Sandor Howard stock in
trade. They grind down the rims of fine crystal goblets to remove chips.
The risk of breakage is always there, but this shop's batting average is
high.

HANDBAGS

ART BAG / 735 Madison Avenue between 64th and 65th Streets
Monday through Friday 9:00 to 5:45, Saturday 9:00 to 4:00
744–2720

Fixing pocketbooks is their bag. Art Bag's repairs are well done, for
which they really deserve credit—but your credit rating needs to be high
to afford the fixing here. You can often buy one of the bags they sell for
less money than it takes to fix your own.

JEWELRY

B. HARRIS AND SONS / 25 1/2 East 61st Street between
Madison and Park Avenues / Monday through Saturday 9:30 to
5:30 / 755–6455

When you take your valuables to Mr. Harris, you feel they are in good
hands. Along with the excellent repairs and fair prices, they carry a small
collection of traditional jewelry.

*LEE JEWELRY / 57 East 59th Street between Madison and Park
Avenues / Monday, Tuesday, Wednesday, Friday, 8:30 to 6:00,
Thursday, 8:30 to 8:30, Saturday, 10:00 to 5:00 / 753–7614*

We all like Lee; he's perpetually cheerful and is undaunted by any fix-it
job, no matter how minor or complex. He not only solders chains, repairs
jewelry and watches, restrings pearls, and does engraving quickly, but he
sometimes does it while you wait. With a bit of persuasion he can
re-"pair" a mateless earring. The store sells inexpensive watches, earrings,
chains, bands and other accessories, but we seek him out for his excellent
repair work.

SHOES

*JIM'S SHOE REPAIRING AND HAT RENOVATING
CO. / 50 East 59th Street between Madison and Park Avenues
Monday through Friday, 8:00 to 6:00, Saturday 8:00 to 4:00
355–8259*

At Jim's you can get your shoes shined or repaired while you wait. They
do an excellent job of half-soling or whole-soling, repairing heels, adding
lifts, inserting metatarsal pads and inner soles. They'll also fix belts and
handbag straps. In addition, here you can purchase shoe stretchers, polish
and even plastic rain boots.

SILVER

*CLIFF SILVER CO. / 159 East 55th Street between Lexington and
Third Avenues / Monday through Friday, 8:00 to 5:00 / 753–8348*

Major and minor restorations for sterling silver and vermeil are their
business. In addition to re-silvering, re-gilting and de-denting, they'll
re-solder and patch silver pieces worth saving—and what isn't at today's
prices?

Florists

In our City of concrete, steel and glass, flowers, trees and plants become visual delights. We New Yorkers plant trees and gardens behind our brownstone houses and pot them on our terraces and in our lobbies. We put hanging baskets in the windows of apartments and pay for the planting of trees and flowers on city streets. City, state, federal and private funds are used to help keep our parks green. Business organizations, nonprofit charitable organizations and just plain citizens place planters on sidewalks and seasonally put Christmas trees and flowering plants all around the town.

Our love and need for green things probably explains the number of excellent florist shops that grace New York. Naturally some are more expensive than others—price generally depending upon location of the shop, originality of arrangements, freshness and quality of flowers.

ALPINE FLORISTS / *999 Lexington Avenue at 72nd Street*
Monday through Saturday 9:00 to 7:00 / 879–6933

Alpine Florists will find you the perfect natural Christmas tree or make it so by wiring on branches to achieve absolute symmetry. Perfection is costly when you have them enhance the tree with lights and decorations. If you keep lights and baubles, they'll gladly put them on the tree you buy from them year after year after year . . .

JEAN JACQUES BLOOS, LTD. / *1025 Lexington Avenue*
between 73rd and 74th Streets / Monday through Friday 9:00 to
5:30, Saturday 9:00 to early afternoon / 861–0575

Jean Jacques Bloos is a very chic and commensurately priced florist that specializes in unique arrangements. A favorite is a basket filled with miniature ferns growing out of a bed of moss with a single flowering bulb or orchid in the center. Mr. Bloos designs party rooms and tables. He has special tablecloths for rent (at $15 and up) and if you want something even more unusual, he will make it to order.

BOUQUETS À LA CARTE / 222 East 83rd Street between
  Second and Third Avenues / Monday through Friday 9:30 to 5:30
  Saturday 10:00 to 1:00 / 535–3720

Roy Strickland is the owner of Bouquets à la Carte and the person to
order flowers from for a special occasion. Tell him your mother is ill, and
one of his sweet and charmingly nostalgic bouquets will brighten her day.
Bouquets à la Carte is best known for its basket of flowers tied to a
giant-sized helium balloon with trailing streamers, individualized with
"Happy Birthday," "Bon Voyage," "Get Well" or any appropriate
expression of your choice. It's a very good show, and the price is
determined by the balloon's anchor (brandy, champagne, flowers). The
cheapest is $25.

BURNETT BROS. / 92 Chambers Street between Broadway and
  Church Street / Monday through Friday 8:30 to 4:30 / 227–6138

Burnett Brothers is a good source for seeds and bulbs. Send for their
catalogue.

CHRISTATOS & KOSTER / Madison Avenue at 63rd Street
  Monday through Friday 8:00 to 5:00, Saturday 8:00 to 2:00
  838–0022

Christatos and Koster has an enormous variety of cut flowers in stock
and many arrangements to choose from when you need flowers in a
hurry. They specialize in house plants—particularly flowering ones—and
they are very nice people to do business with. Prices are competitive.

CITY GARDENER, INC. / 105 West 55th Street between Sixth
  and Seventh Avenues / by appointment / 777–8810

The City Gardener will do anything and everything connected with a
city garden, be it a single window box, a terrace, a backyard or rooftop
garden, an office oasis, whatever. After everything is in place they will
maintain the planting, and they are experts at combatting the many
menaces to city flora. One can visit their office to see drawings and
portfolios of past work. The staff is amiable and the rates are reasonable,
in fact, less than most of their competitors (labor: $15 per hour or any
part thereof).

*PAMELA DUVAL / 680 Madison Avenue between 61st and 62nd
Streets / Monday through Saturday 9:30 to 5:30 / 751–2126*

Pamela Duval has a fascinating collection of silk flowers that survive
summer wilting, if you can survive the prices.

*FERNERY / 1198 Madison Avenue between 87th and 88th Streets
Monday through Saturday 9:00 to 6:00 / 289–9063*

The Fernery is known for its special arrangements of unusual botanical
species. Mrs. Ford, in her White House days, used to call on The
Fernery to "do" the tables on state occasions.

*H. CARL HOLPP & CO., INC. / 823 Lexington Avenue at 63rd
Street / Monday through Friday 8:00 to 5:00, Saturday 8:00 to
2:00 / 838–6977*

This neighborhood florist specializes in potted plants, with heavy
emphasis on the flowering variety. Their selection of cut flowers is
limited, but you can count on their quality and freshness. Arrangements
are not their forte, but if you can do them yourself, you get masses of
blooms for your money.

*MACDONALD FORBES / Hotel Carlyle / 981 Madison Avenue
between 76th and 77th Streets / Monday through Friday 9:00 to
5:00 / 628–2250*

This is a florist that has had its ups and downs, but now it's really good
again. You buy arrangements here, not cut flowers, and you get beautiful
ones; each bouquet is a breathtaking variety of colors and blooms and
rarely will you see another like it. Their containers are *not* pedestrian,
like those of some other florists we know.

*RONALDO MAIA FLOWERS / 27 East 67th Street between
Madison and Park Avenues / Monday through Friday 9:00 to 6:00,
Saturday 10:00 to 5:00 / 288–1049*

Ronaldo Maia's specialties are terra cotta–woven and trompe l'oeil cache
pots and baskets filled with flowers. The potpourri is divine. If expense is
no object, have him do his fabulous centerpiece(s) for dinner parties.

*REX RICHARDS / 782 Lexington Avenue at 61st Street / Monday
through Saturday 9:00 to 7:00 / 838-2370*

For the Bloomingdale crowd, Rex Richards sells newpaper-wrapped
flowers by the bunch from his sidewalk stand. Inside, the shop is a jungle
of baskets, dried flowers and a few flowering plants. You would never
guess by the looks of things that Rex Richards has one of the most
exclusive clienteles in town. He is their florist for all seasons, reasons and
occasions. His flowers are bought with customers in mind, so they are
always fresh and of great quality. He arranges them in baskets, bottles or
the usual florist containers for his walk-in trade, but for his special
customers, he picks up, fills and redelivers the odd piece of fine
porcelain, old silver or Bacarrat crystal that graces their mantels and
tables.

A handy man to have around when you're throwing a party, Richards
throws himself into the theme and no effort seems too much. His rates
are very fair.

*TERRESTRIS / 409 East 60th Street between First and York Avenues
Monday through Sunday 8:00 A.M. to 11:00 P.M. / 758-8181*

Yes, we have a greenhouse in New York and it's a penthouse, at that.
The name is Terrestris and it's solely devoted to plants and trees. The
vast selection of full-grown trees is perfect for lobbies, offices and sparsely
furnished apartments. If it's a thank-you present you're after—think
smaller, and you'll find Terrestris has a marvelous collection of all kinds
of plants, flowering and just plain green. Prices are competitive.

Furniture

Whether it's any or every Louis, the Bauhaus, the English Queens, chrome-and-steel contemporary or summer-house wicker that suits your furniture fancy, you'll find it in abundance around Manhattan. For the something old, see Antique Dealers, Auction Houses (pages 5 and 14), or see for yourself up and down East 57th Street, Second, Third and Madison Avenues from 58th to 86th, or see furniture on the streets in New York's special "estate" district on Broadway around East 11th Street. In the estate district you have to buy strictly "as is," so go securely armed with your own expertise or that of a decorator. For the something new you might head first to the furniture display rooms in the department stores or, if you still have your decorator in tow, to the Decorator and Designers building at 979 Third Avenue. For the something borrowed, if you have no obliging relatives, you can rent a chair, a desk or a whole roomful of furniture on a long or short term basis. For the something blue . . . well . . . see Wallpaper and Paint (page 214).

DEPARTMENT STORES

The department stores which carry both antique and new furniture are: Altman's, Bloomingdale's, Lord & Taylor's and Macy's. For addresses and hours, see pages 64–69.

FURNITURE STORES

> DOOR STORE / 210 East 51st Street between Second and Third
> Avenues / Monday through Friday 10:00 to 7:00, Saturday 10:00
> to 6:00, Sunday noon to 5:00 / 753–2280

The Door Store carries basic, no-frills, contemporary furniture with
reproductions of famous classics like the Parsons table, campaign chests
and a whole collection of well-known chair designs. They manage to keep
their prices low because they're dealing in mass, but there's plenty of
class.

> W. J. SLOANE, INC. / Fifth Avenue at 38th Street / Monday
> through Saturday 9:30 to 5:30, Sunday and holidays noon to 5:00
> 695–3800

The many floors of this store devoted to both antique and new furniture
make it a good place for educating your furniture eye and getting a
bird's-eye view of the current home furnishing industry. Sloane's sells odd
pieces of furniture or suites, whichever suits your need. Their
merchandise is good, their decorating advice faultless and their prices
compatible.

INDOOR-OUTDOOR FURNITURE

> MAYHEW-COPLEY, LTD. / 509 Park Avenue between 59th and
> 60th Streets / Monday through Friday 9:00 to 5:20, Saturday 11:00
> to 5:00 / 759–8120

This store caters to the al fresco way of life. Its wares in the furniture
line—made of plastic and wrought iron, aluminum, bamboo, wicker and
rattan—are perfect for outdoors and sun porches, playrooms and bars. To
go with all this informality, Mayhew stocks ceramic everythings. They
also have some fine French porcelain and pottery, a wide variety of
laminated plastic place mats with matching cotton napkins, and a good
supply of stainless steel flatware.

WALTER'S WICKER WONDERLAND / 991 Second Avenue
between 52nd and 53rd Streets / Monday through Friday 9:30 to
5:30 / 758-0472

Walter has a veritable wonderland of wicker and rattan furniture, ranging from laundry baskets to headboards, to lamps and lamp tables, to chests, to mirrors, to benches, to chairs, to sofas, to card tables, to—you get the idea! Items come unfinished, but can be varnished or painted at a slight additional cost. They cater both to decorators and to the retail trade.

RENTALS

APARTMENT FURNITURE RENTALS / 139 East 57th Street
at Lexington Avenue / Monday through Friday 9:30 to 6:00,
Saturday 9:00 to 4:00 / 751-1530

You can rent furniture and rugs by the roomful here at a monthly rate. There is a decorator on hand to guide your selection. Minimum rental is for a three-month period with a one-year security deposit required, which still makes renting cheaper than buying.

UNFINISHED

FURNITURE- IN- THE- RAW / 1017 Second Avenue between
53rd and 54th Streets / Monday, Tuesday, Wednesday, Friday
10:00 to 7:00, Thursday 10:00 to 9:00, Saturday 11:00 to 6:00,
Sunday noon to 6:00 / 355-7373

The raw furniture here consists of chests, desks, tables, bookcases and benches. You can take it home and finish it yourself, or they'll complete it for you in a variety of colors or finishes. The biggest saving is for the do-it-yourselfer.

Gift Shops

While a gift can be anything from a box of candy to a fabulous diamond necklace, for some unknown reason the shops that bear the name "gift" mostly carry things for the home. The luxe of the luxe gift shops are Tiffany and Cartier, closely followed by the department stores. Here we describe the small shops that are individualized by the stamp of their owner's personality and are a source of countless unusual gift items. This unique quality, of course, is usually not inexpensive. Their price range is enormous.

CACHE-CACHE / 758 Madison Avenue between 65th and 66th Streets / Monday through Friday 10:00 to 5:30, Saturday 11:00 to 5:00 / 744–6886; 744–7060

One of the owners of this special gift shop is Charlotte Ford, which is only one of the reasons it's a favorite haunt of ours. Cache-Cache has a superb array of gifts ranging from baskets (see page 17), tableware, cache pots, picture frames, place mats, cocktail napkins, coasters and other decorative or useful items. The Porthault pattern on their linen items was designed for Cache-Cache and is theirs exclusively. In fact, their specialty is made-to-order table linens.

CARDEL, LTD. / 615 Madison Avenue between 58th and 59th Streets / Monday through Friday 9:45 to 5:45, Saturday 9:45 to 5:30 / 753–8880

See page 58.

DIANE LOVE / 851 Madison Avenue between 70th and 71st Streets Monday through Saturday 10:00 to 5:30 / 879–6997

The things we like best at Diane Love's are her silk flower arrangements, which she'll put into anything from a straw basket to a Ming vase. She also specializes in lovely shell-covered boxes and picture frames, a handful of antiques she picks up in her travels and elegant brocade purses.

LUCIDITY / 775 Madison Avenue at 66th Street / Monday through Friday 10:30 to 6:30, Saturday 11:00 to 6:00 / 861–7000

Everything you ever wanted in Lucite, and probably many things you'll never want. And, what's more, the Lucite items come in lots of colors.

MAYHEW-COPLEY, LTD. / 509 Park Avenue between 59th and 60th Streets / Monday through Friday 9:00 to 5:20, Saturday 11:00 to 5:00 / 759–8120

See page 88.

MEDITERRANEAN SHOP / 876 Madison Avenue between 71st and 72nd Streets / Monday through Friday 10:00 to 5:30 879–3120

The Mediterranean Shop specializes in desk items covered in Florentine papers. Also featured is a selection of Portuguese pottery, silk embroidered down-filled cushions, hand-embroidered cocktail napkins and other appealing items, mostly handmade from Mediterranean countries.

MARCO POLO GIFT SHOP / 855 Lexington Avenue between 64th and 65th Streets / Monday through Friday 11:00 to 6:00, Saturday noon to 5:00 / 861–6446

More often than not, you'll find items here you can't resist buying for yourself, as well as for friends. Marco Polo's stocks practical housewares such as Cuisinarts, sea salt and pepper grinders, along with aprons emblazoned with sassy sayings such as, "For this I got a college education." It also carries pretty dishes, glasses, practical soufflé and quiche casseroles and checked napkins tied together in wicker baskets. Try it, you'll like it.

SCULLY & SCULLY / 506 Park Avenue between 59th and 60th Streets / Monday through Friday 9:30 to 5:30, Saturday 10:00 to 5:00 / 755–2590

See page 59.

CAROLE STUPELL, LTD. / 61 East 57th Street between Madison and Park Avenues / Monday through Saturday 9:30 to 6:00 / 260–3100

Very highly styled ornate china, crystal, silver and other items for gifting. Make sure the present you select is in stock, or be prepared to wait months for delivery.

Gifts Personalized

Personalizing gifts is an instant "care" package which clearly shows the recipients your gifts are just for them. There are many ways to personalize a present: make it yourself, have it initialed or, if you are in N.Y., N.Y., there are a host of other ways, some of which we've listed below.

CAKES

> *CREATIVE CAKES / 400 East 74th Street between First and York Avenues / Monday through Friday by appointment, Saturday 12:00 to 4:30 / 794–9811*

For this ultimate in edible personalized gifts, see page 142.

CHAINS

> *BLOOMINGDALE'S / Lexington Avenue between 59th and 60th Streets / Monday and Thursday 9:45 to 9:00, Tuesday, Wednesday, Friday, Saturday 9:45 to 6:00 / 355–5900*

Bloomingdale's has miles of chains, some of which they sell by the inch. Their gold, gold-filled and gold-plated chains can be had in a variety of weights, link sizes and lengths. While you stand and wait they will make up a necklace, bracelet, key chain or even ankle bracelet—and to make it even more personal, they just happen to have a supply of initials (also gold) to add to the chain of your choice. All of which makes it possible to have a last-minute gift appear to have been long planned. Surprisingly, all this personalization doesn't add to the cost.

CHOCOLATE

> KRON CHOCOLATIER / 764 Madison Avenue between 65th and
> 66th Streets / second floor / Tuesday through Saturday 10:00 to
> 6:00 / 288–9259

See page 44.

COLLAGES

> PERSONALITY COLLAGES / 5 East 85th Street at Fifth Avenue
> by appointment / 757–6300

Penny Ekstein and Joan Halpern, two talented women, call their collages
"Your Own Hangups." They make a highly unusual, thoughtful gift for a
very special occasion for a friend, employer, love or whomever. Once
you've ordered this gift, the subject's interests, habits, experiences, et al.,
are researched and the resultant collage is an instant life history, nicely
framed. Advance notice of three to four weeks is needed. The collages
start at $500, with size and complexity determining the price.

MUSICAL MESSAGES

> MUSIC BOX, INC. / 39 Eighth Avenue, Brooklyn, New York 11217
> mail or phone orders accepted / 857–1821

Remember the old-fashioned singing telegram? In a burst of nostalgia,
the Music Box has brought it back in a modern version. You provide the
information, they rhyme your thoughts, set them to music, then phone
your special someone (anywhere in the continental U.S.A.) and sing your
message—twice! Orders may be placed by phone, but the Music Box
needs one week's advance notice. The cost is $15. For another $5 they
will send a tape cassette in addition to the phoned message.

SLIPPERS

*DUNHILL TAILORED CLOTHES / 65 East 57th Street
between Madison and Park Avenues / Monday through Saturday
9:00 to 5:00 / 355–0050*

To fancify feet of some man you fancy, Dunhill will add his initials to
the black, bottle green or wine velvet slippers they always stock. Allow
about a week for delivery and be prepared to spend around $60.

T-SHIRTS

*DECO-DANCE / 718 Lexington Avenue between 58th and 59th
Streets / Monday, Thursday, Friday 11:00 to 7:30, Tuesday,
Wednesday, Saturday 11:00 to 6:00 / 355–0228*

While you wait, you can immortalize any word ("ouch"), a provocative
saying ("Kiss me, I'm Irish"), or any name ("Alfred E. Neuman") on a
T-shirt. And with the craze for T-shirts showing no sign of abatement,
this can be a last-minute gift that looks like it took months of planning.
Even a snapshot can be T-shirted in three days.

*P & J STATIONERY / 882 First Avenue at 50th Street / Monday
through Friday 7:00 to 8:00, Saturday 7:00 to 7:00, Sunday 7:00 to
2:00 / 755–1988*

Like Deco-Dance (see above), P & J Stationery emblazons T-shirts and
other items with personal messages and photos. We include them
(though they are a little off the beaten track) because they are open on
Sunday.

Glassware (Crystal)

In 1939 Henri Soulé opened the fabulous French restaurant, Pavillon, at the World's Fair and introduced a larger-than-life wine goblet made especially for him by Baccarat. Soulé proclaimed that only in these large glasses could fine, rare red wines breathe properly. Soulé spoke and the world listened, and so today the "Pavillon" glass and reasonable facsimiles thereof can be found on tables everywhere. The adaptations, sometimes known as "the all-purpose wineglass," are available in every quality of glassware. The less expensive version is stocked by gift shops, department, hardware, and even five-and-ten-cent stores. For fine crystal glasses for wine, water, whiskey or whatever, the department stores, Cardel, Cartier, Tiffany, Jensen, Ginori and Plummer McCutcheon all have good though limited supplies. There are two shops in N.Y., N.Y., however, devoted exclusively to crystal and they are described below.

BACCARAT, INC. / 55 East 57th Street between Madison and Park Avenues / Monday through Saturday 9:30 to 5:30 / 826-4100

Baccarat has crystal everything, from carafes to candlesticks, ashtrays, bowls, dishes, vases, and glasses for water, whiskey and whatever, plus stemware for wine—including the authentic Pavillon model. The imported French crystal is lovely to look at but expensive to buy.

STEUBEN GLASS / Fifth Avenue at 56th Street / Monday through Saturday 9:30 to 5:30 / 752-1441

Kings, Queens, Presidents, Governors, Mayors and just plain citizens (plain but rich) collect Steuben animals and its other unique glass sculptures (all made in N.Y.). While other stores sell Steuben stemware, only at Steuben's Fifth Avenue shop will you find a large display of its museum-quality stemware, vases and decorative pieces. Steuben invites browsers, so even those who can't afford to buy can look.

Handbags

Each department store has its in-house handbag specialty shop: for example, both Bergdorf Goodman and Bloomingdale's have a Bottega Veneta Boutique; at Bonwit Teller a whole shop is devoted to Hermès; Saks features Judith Leiber, Sacha and Vuitton. The leather shops—Gucci, Mädler and Lederer—all have a huge assortment of women's handbags. There is also a group of small specialty handbag shops on and just off Madison Avenue that we think have good-looking and unusual selections.

ART BAG / 735 Madison Avenue between 64th and 65th Streets
Monday through Friday 9:00 to 5:45, Saturday 9:00 to 4:00
744–2720

We use this shop primarily for repairs (see page 81), but it also sells new handbags—generally copies of very expensive imported bags at copy-cat prices.

HENRI BETRIX, INC. / 699 Madison Avenue at 61st Street
Monday through Saturday 9:30 to 5:00 / 838–8120

Henri Betrix stands for quality in handbags—and they mostly stock bags made by hand. The prices start high and go higher for made-to-order work. Before you invest in a Betrix Bag, be sure it's in a color and style you really like because it will be so well made it will last you a lifetime.

ROBERTA DI CAMERINO / 645 Fifth Avenue at 51st Street
Monday through Saturday 10:00 to 6:00 / 355–7600

America's first branch of the famous Venetian cut-velvet artist has a dazzling array of trompe l'oeil cut-velvet pocketbooks for day and evening. There is also luggage and clothing (see page 35), all very expensive.

JACOMO / 25 East 61st Street between Madison and Park Avenues
Monday through Friday 9:30 to 5:30, Saturday 9:30 to 5:00
832–9038

French handbags beautifully designed in top quality leathers and fabrics.
Very expensive, but elegant and distinctive-looking. Custom-made bags
also available.

LA JEUNESSE / 800B Madison Avenue between 67th and 68th
Streets / Monday through Friday 10:00 to 7:00, Saturday 10:00 to
6:00 / 988–6967

Art deco frames are used in the construction of their splendid new
handbags. *Très chic. Très cher.*

LESTER BAGS / 669 Madison Avenue at 61st Street / Monday
through Saturday 9:30 to 5:00 / 838–5653

Good-looking imported and domestic bags, including the famous
Nantucket basket, are reasonably priced. Lester Bags also carries a wide
assortment of leather goods. Backgammon sets are their biggest game,
along with novelty items suitable for stocking-stuffing. For
handbag-stuffing, they'll make fitted leather or fabric covers to protect
gold lighters, compacts and cigarette cases.

MÄDLER PARK AVENUE / 450 Park Avenue at 57th Street
Monday through Saturday 9:00 to 5:30 / 688–5045

Big store, big selection of imported handbags and leather goods, big
prices.

J. S. SUAREZ / 680 Madison Avenue at 62nd Street / Monday
through Friday 10:00 to 6:00, Saturday 10:00 to 5:00 / 759–9443

A good selection of imported handbags, including excellent copies of
designer bags, ranging from the reasonable to expensive. Some items
found in department stores are sold here at 20% to 30% less.

Handkerchiefs

With the demise of convent-trained stitchers, the modern handkerchief is no longer a thing of beauty, but merely a serviceable accessory. (Although, as you will see, for a wedding day you can have one of the old-time tear-catchers duplicated at a staggering price.) Men's serviceable handkerchiefs worth the price of initialing are similarly hard to come by. While you can find handkerchiefs in nearly every department store and even in five-and-tens, we've limited our comments to the few specialty shops that carry the better than average variety.

E. BRAUN & COMPANY / 717 Madison Avenue between 63rd and 64th Streets / Monday through Friday 9:30 to 5:30, Saturday 9:30 to 5:00 / 833–0650

Here's where both men and women find fine linen handkerchiefs; some already embroidered, others plain, suitable for either hand or machine embroidery. And this is the store that will copy the handkerchief of your dreams at a dreamy price—would you believe $50 for *one* handkerchief?

DUNHILL TAILORED CLOTHES / 65 East 57th Street between Madison and Park Avenues / Monday through Saturday 9:00 to 5:00 / 355–0050

Have men's linen handkerchiefs; will monogram, but only from stock models. Have silk pocket handkerchiefs, will coordinate with their neckties. Perfect spot for prosperous patrons with top taste.

LERON / 745 Fifth Avenue between 57th and 58th Streets / Monday through Friday 9:30 to 6:00, Saturday 9:30 to 5:00 / 753–6700

Linen handkerchiefs for both sexes are available at Leron. They monogram and have models to chose from; in some instances, they will copy monograms of a customer's own design. Nothing is cheap at Leron, but at least you are paying for quality.

SULKA & COMPANY / 711 Fifth Avenue at 55th Street / Monday through Saturday 9:30 to 5:30 / 980–5200

Hand-embroidered monogramming on linen handkerchiefs is a $ulka $ervice. They will copy a monogram or furnish samples to choose from. Also, they have a selection of silk pocket-handkerchiefs to complement their ties.

Hardware

Since we are not "handymen," we are never in the market for tools of various trades, so we do not shop in many specialized hardware emporiums that dot our City. Those we list below are the ones that fill our ordinary household needs—for more technical hardware centers, check New York's Yellow Pages.

GRACIOUS HOME / 1220 Third Avenue between 70th and 71st Streets / Monday and Thursday 8:30 to 9:00, Tuesday, Wednesday, Friday and Saturday 8:30 to 7:00 / 535–2033

A serious hardware store where the inventory is as organized as a supermarket and the sales personnel is pleasant and helpful, whether you are searching for carpet tacks or major appliances—both of which they have, incidentally, as well as everything in between.

HUNRATH / 153 East 57th Street between Lexington and Third Avenues / Monday through Friday 9:00 to 5:00, Saturday 9:00 to 3:00 / 758–0780

Functional and ornamental hardware is their specialty. You'll find brassware—from reproductions to newly designed doorknobs, hinges, knockers, drawer pulls, plates for electric switches, and the like. Also, an unalloyed selection of other luxurious household items. This hardware store can be bypassed if you are just in the market for run-of-the-mill nuts and bolts.

LEXINGTON HARDWARE AND ELECTRIC CO., INC.
797 Lexington Avenue between 61st and 62nd Streets / Monday through
Saturday 8:00 to 5:45 / 838–5386

A haven for the handyman and also for amateur do-it-yourselfers. This happy hodgepodge of a hardware store has everything but aisle room. From nuts and bolts to saws and scissors, from electric wire to electric converters, from hair dryers to foot massagers, to say nothing of their refrigerator containers, and their dishes, pots, pans, glassware, tiles, lining paper, spackle, paint, paint brushes—you name it and they've got it, including keys made on the premises.

Hats

Every department store has a hat bar and that's where we buy our "town" hats—be they fur or straw, knitted or anything in between. Our sources for "sporting" hats, and those for special occasions, such as weddings, we've listed below, along with places most men we know buy their hats.

Irish Hats and Caps

IRISH PAVILION / 130 East 57th Street between Lexington and
Park Avenue / Monday through Saturday, 10:30 A.M. to midnight
759–9041

Made-to-Order Ladies' Hats

DON MARSHALL, INC. / 18 East 53rd Street between Fifth and Madison Avenues / Monday through Friday 9:30 to 5:00 758–1686

Men's Hats

CAVANAGH HATS / 400 Madison Avenue at 47th Street / Monday through Saturday 9:00 to 5:30 / 751–8160

Ski Caps

SCANDINAVIAN SKI SHOP / 40 West 57th Street between Fifth and Sixth Avenues / Monday through Friday 9:30 to 6:00, Saturday 9:30 to 5:00 / 757–8524

Straw Hats

AZUMA / 666 Lexington Avenue between 55th and 56th Streets Monday through Saturday 10:00 to 9:00 / 752–0599
251 East 86th Street between Second and Third Avenues Monday through Friday 10:00 to 10:00, Saturday 10:00 A.M. to 10:30 P.M., Sunday 11:00 to 7:30 / 369–4928
415 Fifth Avenue between 37th and 38th Streets / Monday through Saturday 10:00 to 6:30 / 889–4310

Tennis Hats

TENNIS LADY, INC. / 765 Madison Avenue between 65th and 66th Streets / Monday through Friday 10:00 to 6:00, Saturday 10:30 to 5:30 / 535–8601

Hayrides

See page 164.

Horses

BETTING

OFF-TRACK BETTING CORPORATION For information about Off-Track Betting: 221–5451; customer service: 221–5461

Locations: *Grand Central Station*
575 Lexington Avenue at 51st Street
16 East 52nd Street at Fifth Avenue
150 East 58th Street at Third Avenue
56 East 59th Street between Park and Madison Avenues

RACE TRACKS

AQUEDUCT RACE TRACK / Rockaway Boulevard at 110th Street, Ozone Park, Queens / January 2nd through May 1st, June 30th through July 31st / 641–4700

BELMONT PARK RACE TRACK / Hempstead Turnpike and Plainfield Avenue, Elmont, Long Island / May 3rd through June 28th, August 30th through October 23rd / 516–641–4700

*ROOSEVELT RACEWAY (trotters)   Westbury, Long Island
January 2nd through March 6th, May 18th through July 17th,
October 18th through December 11th / 516–746–6000*

*YONKERS RACEWAY (trotters)   Yonkers, New York / March 8th
through May 17th, July 19th through October 16th, December
13th through December 31st / 914–968–4200*

RIDING

*CLAREMONT RIDING ACADEMY / 175 West 89th Street
between Columbus and Amsterdam Avenues / for lesson schedules,
fees and appointment: 724–5100*

Riding here is in an indoor ring; those qualified may ride in Central
Park, which is a block and a half away. The riding paths are usually
uncrowded and bucolic.

If instead of riding *on* a horse, you choose to ride *behind* one, just
trot over to Grand Army Plaza at 59th and Fifth Avenue and take a ride
through Central Park or other selected routes, at rates set by the City of
New York.

RIDING CLOTHES

See page 198.

Hospitals

There are many public and private hospitals in New York. For
a few emergency hospital clinics, see page 75.

Hotels

N.Y. hotels fall into three categories: the fashionable luxurious, the smaller residential and the large commercial hotel.

FAVORITE SUPER-LUXURY HOTELS

Our famous deluxe hotels all offer pretty much the same attractive rooms, good service and the usual amenities—including good room service, dining rooms, pleasant bars and fine banquet facilities, with prices to match the extensive services provided.

HOTEL CARLYLE / 35 East 76th Street at Madison Avenue 744–1600

This superb small hotel is right in the heart of Madison Avenue art, auction and boutique country. It has pleasant dining rooms where private conversations are possible at lunch, tea or dinner. The Café Carlyle features entertainers, such as Bobby Short, and is one of the more popular nightspots in town.

PARK LANE HOTEL / 36 Central Park South between Fifth and Sixth Avenues, with an entrance on 58th Street / 371–4000

The Park Lane is a beautiful hotel. The newest in the group, it therefore has the most modern facilities. It offers a breathtaking view of Central Park, and the garage on the premises means faster car service.

PIERRE HOTEL / Fifth Avenue at 61st Street / 838–8000

This is the elegant home of many rich New Yorkers who rent their apartments on a yearly basis. The best and most expensive suites are on the higher floors with a view of Central Park. The Café Pierre offers good dining facilities and piano music as well. Excellent banquet rooms, including the old Cotillion Room for larger parties.

PLAZA HOTEL / Fifth Avenue at 59th Street / 759–3000

The Plaza, famous as the home of Eloise, is the grand old lady of New York hotels. It had a recent face-lift inside and out, so the decor is fresh and sparkling. Aside from the Waldorf, the Plaza offers the greatest variety of public rooms, entertainment, boutiques, and similar services. It's the home of Trader Vic's, the Oak Room and Oak Room Bar, the Edwardian Room (wonderful for Sunday Brunch), the Oyster Bar and the Palm Court, which has the most European atmosphere in the City.

REGENCY HOTEL / Park Avenue at 61st Street / 759–4100

Another of the newer entries, which again means more modern rooms, but slightly on the small side. Pleasant dining room and a popular bar. In-house garage here, too.

SHERRY NETHERLAND HOTEL / 781 Fifth Avenue at 59th Street / 355–2800

Although a good number of the suites in this fine, old-time hotel are taken by the year, there are still some transient rooms to be had. Great service, pleasant bar and restaurant where you can brunch, lunch, or dine and watch the Fifth Avenue "parade." Doubles, the private club, is downstairs.

ST. REGIS-SHERATON HOTEL / 2 East 55th Street between Fifth and Madison Avenues / 753–4500

Now a Sheraton hotel, the St. Regis still has remnants of its grandeur of yesteryear. Some of the suites are quite elegant. There are fine public accommodations, good bar, dancing in the Maisonette. The Library and the St. Regis Roof are among the City's most pleasant places for private parties.

WALDORF-ASTORIA HOTEL / Park Avenue between 49th and 50th Streets / 355–3000

The largest and most bustling of the group, the Waldorf still has excellent rooms and the largest variety of dancing, drinking and dining spots, including the best Japanese restaurant in town, Inagiku. Another attraction is the Boutique Row, featuring such shops as Sulka, Mark Cross, Hanae Mori, etc. There is an infinite number of banquet rooms, from the grand Grand Ballroom to dozens of smaller suites for private parties.

WALDORF TOWERS / 50th Street between Lexington and Park Avenues / 355-3100

This is really the residential arm of the Waldorf, but there are some transient suites available. The Towers is probably the best address in town. It is literally connected with the Waldorf proper, so it does not have its own public rooms. The guests generally prefer entertaining in their own private suites.

FINE SMALLER RESIDENTIAL HOTELS

New York's smaller hotels each has its own atmosphere. They cater to transients, but many of them are filled with permanent residents, so it is often difficult to book a room for a short stay. Most of them have dining rooms which are open to the public, and many of them are excellent.

ALGONQUIN HOTEL / 59 West 44th Street between Fifth and Sixth Avenues / 687-4400

Because of its location, this hotel is a favorite of literati and theater people. Once the home of the famous "Round Table," presided over by Dorothy Parker, Alec Woollcott and George S. Kaufman, et al., it is still a magnet for the hungry Broadway-bound at lunch, tea, cocktails and pre- or après-theatre dinner.

BEEKMAN HOTEL / 575 Park Avenue at 63rd Street / 838-4900

The residents of the Beekman Hotel own their apartments and from time to time some of these suites are available for resale. The dining room, Le Perigord Park, one of New York's better-known restaurants, is open to the public for lunch and dinner. Pleasant atmosphere.

CARLTON HOUSE / 680 Madison Avenue between 61st and 62nd Streets / 838-3000

Good, quiet, residential hotel. Unless a sublet is available, rentals are only on a long-term basis. The restaurant, La Folie, is on the Carlton House's 61st Street side. It is open for lunch, dinner and late night discotheque-ing.

DRAKE HOTEL / 440 Park Avenue at 56th Street / 421–0900

Comfortable family hotel. Good dining room with piano music at lunch and dinner. Downstairs is one of the City's first discotheques, Shepheard's.

GOTHAM HOTEL / 700 Fifth Avenue at 55th Street / 247–2200

Perfectly located older hotel for those who want the shops of Fifth Avenue at their doorstep. Recently refurbished, the Gotham caters to transients. Its dining room is open for breakfast, lunch and dinner.

LOMBARDY HOTEL / 111 East 56th Street between Madison and Park Avenues / 753–8600

The Lombardy has hotel rooms and apartments for lease and for sale. It contains one of the city's best restaurants, Laurent, which also has banquet facilities.

LOWELL HOTEL / 28 East 63rd Street between Madison and Park Avenues / 838–1400

The Lowell is a very small, quiet, old-world hotel that caters to both transient and permanent guests. Its restaurant is The Grand Café, an art deco setting open for lunch and dinner.

MAYFAIR HOUSE / 610 Park Avenue at 65th Street / 288–0800

An older hostelry, recently renovated for more comfort and style. The Mayfair houses one of the N.Y. ladies' favorite luncheon places, Le Cirque, which is also very good for dinner.

MIDDLETOWN HOTEL / 148 East 48th Street between Lexington and Third Avenues / 755–3000

Small hotel just redone. It's residential in feeling, and marvelously located for midtown business dealings.

RITZ TOWER HOTEL / 465 Park Avenue at 57th Street 755–5000

Although most of the apartments in the Ritz Towers are owned by the residents, there are a few transient rooms available. There is no public dining room, but the room service is excellent, though unfortunately not available on Sunday, or on Saturday in the summer.

ST. MORITZ HOTEL / 50 Central Park South between Fifth and Sixth Avenues / 755–5800

A favorite with many Europeans. Great view of the Park. Good restaurant. And the site of Rumpelmayer's, where you can satisfy a sweet tooth on the premises or with scrumptious packages to take home.

SHERATON - RUSSELL HOTEL / Park Avenue at 37th Street 685–7676

This hotel makes up for being slightly off the beaten track by the individual and personal services offered. Its restaurant has a faithful male following, and the bar at noon serves large drinks and boasts an inexpensive buffet.

STANHOPE HOTEL / Fifth Avenue at 81st Street / 288–5800

A natural for art lovers, the Stanhope's directly across the street from the Metropolitan Museum of Art and within walking distance of the Jewish, Guggenheim, Whitney and Frick Museums. There is a pleasant sidewalk café for balmy summer days and for watching parades.

U.N. PLAZA HOTEL / 1 United Nations Plaza, 44th Street and First Avenue / 355–3400

This is a brand-new, ultra-modern hotel on the 28th to 38th floors of a multi-purpose building directly across the street from the United Nations. It has its own garage below, and a glass-enclosed swimming pool and tennis court on high. The restaurant, bar and lobby on the ground floor are attractively decorated, and usually teeming with diplomats. All rooms are rented solely on a day-to-day basis.

WARWICK HOTEL / 65 West 54th Street at Sixth Avenue 247–2700

A small, quiet, older hotel, it plays host to myriads of out-of-city department store buyers. The Warwick restaurant is a pleasant place for a quick lunch.

N.Y.'S BIG, BUSTLING, COMMERCIAL HOTELS

The hotels of the third variety serve most New York visitors because of their multiplicity of facilities. Most of them have, for instance, convention and banquet halls, ballrooms, various-sized meeting rooms, night clubs, restaurants, bars, shops and 24-hour-a-day room service. The guests include a cross section of America, from business men and women to families with young children.

AMERICANA HOTEL OF NEW YORK / Seventh Avenue at 52nd Street / 581–1000

BILTMORE HOTEL / 43rd Street at Madison Avenue / 687–7000

ESSEX HOUSE / 160 Central Park South between Sixth and Seventh Avenues / 247–0300

NEW YORK HILTON HOTEL / Sixth Avenue between 53rd and 54th Streets / 586–7000

ROOSEVELT HOTEL / 45 West 45th Street between Madison and Vanderbilt Avenues / 686–9200

STATLER HILTON HOTEL / 401 Seventh Avenue between 32nd and 33rd Streets / 736–5000

SUMMIT HOTEL / 569 Lexington Avenue at 51st Street / 752–7000

Jewelry

If you want to just look at the most fabulous gems in the world, you need only drop in on the Museum of Natural History on Central Park West and 79th Street to visit the new permanent collection. In the basement of the Metropolitan Museum, at Fifth Avenue and 82nd Street, there is another gem exhibition. However, if you're lucky enough to actually be in the market for your own precious jewel, the wares of New York's top jewelers rival the Tower of London's Crown Jewels, and in *our* town they're for sale. Even if the Empress Josephine's tiara doesn't fill the bill, it's fun to see it at the corner of Fifth Avenue and 57th Street in Van Cleef and Arpels's window. And certainly the most famous windows in town are Gene Moore's at Tiffany on the opposite corner.

The center of the U.S. diamond and real jewelry market is on 47th Street between Fifth and Sixth Avenues, and spills onto Sixth Avenue. Many of the shops are wholesale, not retail and, if you really know what you're doing, you can sometimes get a bargain. One note to buyers—with some jewelers, it doesn't hurt to ask for a discount.

When it's costume jewelry you're after, there are stores totally devoted to fabulous fakes. If you still can't find what you want, all the department stores have counters and counters of unprecious gems.

THE REAL THING

BULGARI JEWELERS / Pierre Hotel / Fifth Avenue at 61st Street
Monday through Saturday 10:00 to 5:30 / 486-0086

The Bulgari family is known for providing the finest gems in the world for custom-made jewelry. Their shop in the Pierre Hotel has an excellent sampling of gems from the Bulgari headquarters in Rome to build up your own family collection. In addition, they have *the* status solid gold evening bag, complete with changeable silk tassels in different colors. Most of New York's best-dressed necks sport at least one of Bulgari's distinctive chains.

CARTIER / Fifth Avenue at 52nd Street / Monday through Saturday
10:00 to 5:30 / 753–0111

Ownership has changed hands several times, but Cartier's is still located
in a landmark building—and it still stocks its status symbol "tank"
watch, along with some beautiful jewelry, lovely silver, fine porcelain,
classic gold and silver frames and engraved Christmas cards. Its repair
department will work on good jewelry and watches.

DESEDLE'S INC. / 684 Madison Avenue between 61st and 62nd
Streets / Monday through Saturday 9:00 to 5:30 / 753–5024

For many years the Desedles have been buying old gems and jewelry
from individuals and estates and selling it on Madison Avenue. It's one
of those places that can dig out of its vaults (if they're not already on
display in the gem-packed windows) garnets, pearls, black diamonds,
aquamarines, topaz and other stones too exotic to mention. Or if it's
gold you're after, they have some antique (and second-hand) chains,
watches, bracelets, rings and memorabilia of all kinds. They are aware of
the market, but their prices seem fair.

JERRY GRANT, LTD. / 137 East 57th Street between Lexington
and Park Avenues / Monday through Saturday noon to 6:00,
Thursday noon to 9:00 / 371–9769

Jerry Grant designs and adapts his own jewelry. He and his wife run this
store that specializes in semi-precious stones, but which also has a good
sprinkling of the more precious ones.

JAMES ROBINSON, INC. / 12 East 57th Street between Fifth and
Madison Avenues / Monday through Friday 10:00 to 6:00,
Saturday 10:30 to 5:00 / 752–6166

If you have money growing on a tree, you can spend it on the most
beautiful antique jewelry here.

SEAMAN SCHEPPS / 485 Park Avenue at 58th Street / Monday
through Thursday 9:15 to 4:45, Friday 9:15 to 3:45 / 753–9520

Seaman Schepps uses a dazzling array of semi-precious stones and
materials—lapis, coral, topaz, ivory, wood, onyx, baroque pearls, emeralds
and sapphires, to name a few—to set in uniquely designed rings,
necklaces, bracelets and earrings. Many a Greenwich ear sports their
gold-wrapped shell. Their jewelry is high fashion and fairly modestly
priced.

TIFFANY & CO. / 727 Fifth Avenue at 57th Street / Monday
through Saturday 10:00 to 5:30 / 755–8000

Tiffany's is a treasure trove of gold and silver jewelry, watches and fine
gems that run from very, very expensive to reasonably expensive. The
clocks, crystal, silver, china and stationery are all of the highest quality.
The jewelry and watch repair departments are efficient and cooperative,
but unfortunately they handle only Tiffany-stamped goods. Tiffany has
the jewelry of designers Elsa Peretti and Jean Schlumberger, which are
art objects in themselves. One note to buyers: unless you're a corporation
buying multiple gifts, at Tiffany you can't get a discount no matter
who you are or who you know—with any other jeweler it might pay to
ask.

VAN CLEEF & ARPELS / 746 Fifth Avenue at 57th Street
Monday through Saturday 9:30 to 5:00 / 644–9500

Magnificent, flawless gems plus a dazzling choice of really good pieces of
jewelry in designs ranging from modern to antique. They have diamonds,
emeralds, rubies, sapphires and pearls as big as pigeon eggs. Van Cleef &
Arpels are the originators of the invisible setting where the stones are
everything. They also use this setting to particular advantage when
dealing with smaller gems of quality. The pavé flowers are justifiably
world famous.

The Van Cleef & Arpels Boutique is next door in Bergdorf Goodman.
As the word "boutique" implies, it's less expensive, and carries more
14-carat designs than gem carats.

VERDURA, INC. / 5 East 57th Street between Fifth and Madison
Avenues / eleventh floor / Monday through Thursday 9:00 to 5:00,
Friday 9:00 to 4:00 / 265–3227

This small shop makes and sells jewelry of its own designs—usually
limited to one of a kind. Its clientele consists of distinguished,
discriminating taste-setters of the world. Good things that come in small
packages are usually expensive, and Verdura jewels are no exception.

*DAVID WEBB, INC. / 7 East 57th Street between Fifth and
Madison Avenues / Monday through Friday 10:00 to 5:30, open
Saturday, October through December, for Christmas / 421–3030*

There is a rich, beautiful and distinctive look about David Webb jewelry.
His pieces aren't made for little girl graduates; they are massive,
sculptured gold pieces, often set with diamonds. There are zebras and
tigers enameled on gold to wind around wrists and put on fingers and
ears. He combines crystal and gold, and has strung pearls intermingled
with diamonds. The greatness of David Webb's designs is attested to by
the fact that as soon as he makes a piece, some costume jeweler instantly
tries to copy it. His things are beautifully made and we all own some of
them—and love all of them.

*HARRY WINSTON / 718 Fifth Avenue at 56th Street / Monday
through Saturday 10:00 to 5:00 / 245–2000*

Winston is at the top of a list for those searching for unique stones of
gem quality in settings of perfection. His customers are crowned heads of
state, the richest of Greeks and Sheiks, and the wealthiest of the
international set (both titled and untitled). Mr. Winston is constantly on
the lookout for the biggest, the rarest and the best of gems—which he
will set and/or sell unset for those interested in stones for beauty and/or
as an investment.

COSTUME JEWELRY

*CIRO'S OF BOND STREET, INC. / 711 Fifth Avenue between
55th and 56th Streets / Monday through Saturday 9:00 to 5:30
752–0441
6 West 57th Street between Fifth and Sixth Avenues / Monday
through Saturday 9:00 to 5:30 / 581–0767*

Ciro's is for those who can't afford or don't want real jewelry. It looks
real and in fact is usually a copy of a real piece. Generally it is slightly
more expensive than the jewelry for sale in a department store because
it's often Ciro's own thing, designed by them and for them exclusively.

*JOLIE GABOR / 699 Madison Avenue between 62nd and 63rd
Streets / Monday through Saturday 9:30 to 5:30 / 838-3896*

Jolie Gabor, the famous mama of the Gabor sisters, has fondled so many
fine, authentic pieces of jewelry that she reproduces them for those with
a Château Lafite taste and an Almaden budget. The shop carries
crown-jewel-size stones set in necklaces, rings, bracelets and broaches.
Unless you're really rich, they're too big to fool anyone but strangers. At
Gabor's they don't fool around with prices either.

*FLORENCE LUSTIG GEMS / 666 Madison Avenue between
60th and 61st Streets / Monday through Saturday 10:00 to 5:00
421-1540*

Lustigems are magnificent man-made diamonds that look real but are a
lot less expensive. Many New York ladies "safe" their real stuff and get
Lustigem copies to wear everyday. Lustig also has jewels of its own
design that are on display and, like real diamonds, are sold by the carat.

Kitchen and Housewares

Since New York probably has more restaurants to the square inch than any other place in the world, it's little wonder that we also have a group of superb shops devoted to the needs of the professional cook and the aspiring amateur. The department stores, notably Altman's, Bloomingdale's and Macy's, also have areas chock-a-block full of cooking untensils and housewares. So there are lots of choices, whether you are looking for a gift for the person who can't boil water or for cooks as professional as Craig Claiborne and Julia Child.

BRIDGE KITCHENWARE COMPANY / 212 East 52nd Street between Second and Third Avenues / Monday through Friday 9:00 to 5:45, Saturday 10:00 to 5:30 / 688–4220

A midtown hardware store where chefs buy their pots and pans, and restaurateurs buy their wineglasses and table settings wholesale. An amateur cook can buy the same good goods—but at retail prices. Here are all the culinary trappings one could want, and in all sizes too. Even at retail, you won't be overcharged.

LA CUISINIERE, INC. / 867 Madison Avenue between 71st and 72nd Streets / Monday through Saturday 10:00 to 6:00 / 861–4475

An enchanting kitchen shop that stocks copper molds, decanters, measuring spoons and all types of kitchen gadgets, both antique and new.

W. G. LEMMON AND COMPANY / 755 Madison Avenue between 65th and 66th Streets / Monday through Friday 9:00 to 6:00, Saturday 9:00 to 5:00 / 734–4400

An updated version of the hard-to-find old-fashioned neighborhood houseware store, right in the center of boutiqueland. Lemmon stocks new gadgets and old favorites for your home or your home-away-from-home.

POTTERY BARN / 117 East 59th Street between Lexington and Park Avenues / Monday and Thursday 10:00 to 8:30, Tuesday, Wednesday, Friday, Saturday 10:00 to 6:00, Sunday noon to 5:00 838–7130

The Pottery Barn has a huge collection of baskets, kitchenware, tableware, flower pots, cache pots, wooden kitchen implements, etc. Among their specialties are copies of great classic crystal water and wine glasses and goblets at authentically low prices.

666 AVENUE OF THE AMERICAS / between 20th and 21st Streets / Monday through Friday 11:00 to 6:00, Saturday and Sunday 12:30 to 5:00 / 243–6660

This place is so "in" to serious cooks and chefs that it doesn't have a name or a listing in the phone book. What it does have is the definitive supply of cooking utensils, pots, pans and knives for the professional. The fame of this no-name place is spread by word-of-mouth.

Lamps

Most fine sources for lamps that we know about—Donald Hansen, Lighting Associates, Lightolier and Tyndale—are strictly wholesale, and we go to them with a decorator. Otherwise, we buy old crystal, vases, candlesticks, brass, and the like, wherever we find them and have them electrified. The department and furniture stores have large selections of ready-made lighting equipment. If you want contemporary, classic lighting, be it track, wall or free-standing, check out George Kovacs, 831 Madison Avenue.

Leather Goods and Luggage

Anyone who travels a good deal wants luggage that is light-weight, durable, attractive and easily identifiable on the conveyor belt.

Department stores carry name brand luggage, such as American Tourister, Hartman, Lark, Samsonite and Ventura. If you are searching for luggage that is not mass-produced, however, you will need to go to specialty shops.

You'll find smaller leather goods such as desk sets, telephone books, frames, shaving kits, etc., wherever luggage is sold.

T. ANTHONY, LTD. / *772 Madison Avenue at 66th Street*
Monday through Saturday 9:00 to 6:00 / 737–2573

T. Anthony is *the* leather store of old guard New York families. It always has its handsome exclusive luggage in stock, adding new shapes as style dictates. Neither is there any planned obsolescence in the life of the luggage. It lasts and lasts and, if necessary, Anthony will polish and repair its products. In addition, the shop will make luggage to order. Here you will also find a full line of smaller leather items. Since its goods are not mass-produced, they are not mass-priced either.

MARK CROSS / *645 Fifth Avenue between 51st and 52nd Streets*
Monday through Saturday 10:00 to 6:00 / 421–3000

Those with expensive taste can find everything in the way of leather goods at the sign of the "MC": luggage, belts, desk accessories, wallets, purses, card cases, passport cases, note-jotter cases, ties, clocks, shoes, games, leather-covered dictionaries and gloves.

CROUCH & FITZGERALD / 400 Madison Avenue at 48th Street
   Monday through Saturday 9:00 to 6:00 / 755-5888

The ambience of Crouch & Fitzgerald hits you the minute you walk
through the doors and catch the scent of the fine leather. It carries only
top quality luggage, and when it comes to Louis Vuitton, it has the new
and the antique in assorted shapes, boxes and even trunks.

GUCCI SHOPS / 689 Fifth Avenue at 54th Street / 753-8430
      699 Fifth Avenue between 54th and 55th Streets / Monday
   through Saturday 9:30 to 6:00, closed for lunch 12:30 to 1:30
   753-0758

This store is for those who can rise above haughty salespeople, who enjoy
a hassle when making an exchange, and who don't object to the
affectation of a New York store closing for an hour at lunchtime. Gucci's
luggage and leather goods are famous for high quality and design. The
double "G" belt, the classic Gucci loafer and anything else decorated
with the Gucci signature are status symbols easily spotted throughout the
world.

HERMÈS / 57th Street entrance of Bonwit Teller, 721 Fifth Avenue
   Monday through Saturday 10:00 to 6:00, Thursday 10:00 to 8:00
   751-3182

The small beachhead on 57th Street of the famous Hermès shop in Paris
does not carry its name brand luggage, but if you know what you want
they will special order it for you. This jewel of a shop does stock—
among the silk scarves and ties, oversize animal-print turkish towels,
handbags and ready to wear—a good sampling of small leather goods:
wallets, change purses, belts, card cases and an English-style saddle, if
that's what you're in the market for. For an idea of the price range, the
most inexpensive leather belt is $90, and the rest goes up dramatically
from there.

MÄDLER PARK AVENUE / 450 Park Avenue at 57th Street
Monday through Saturday 9:00 to 5:30 / 688-5045

This very old German company has put its roots down on the corner of
57th and Park. Mädler's N.Y. shop has a choice selection of luggage and
many smaller leather items, including a good collection of briefcases.
Everything in this attractive modern shop is made by craftsmen in
Germany and Italy.

LOUIS VUITTON BOUTIQUE / at Saks Fifth Avenue, 611
Fifth Avenue between 49th and 50th Streets / main floor
Monday through Saturday 10:00 to 6:00, Thursday 10:00 to 8:30
753-4000

"He owns Louis Vuitton luggage" was the way novelist John O'Hara
would paint an instant word portrait of a discriminating rich man. Louis
Vuitton still stands for taste, quality and durability. It used to be a
symbol of old money, solely for those who could afford the beautiful
handmade boxes, bags, trunks and heavy cases. Today the "LV"
signature still costs a lot of money and is still well made, but now
everybody who's anybody, or who aspires to be, can find the famed
French signature on something they can afford at the Saks Fifth Avenue
Vuitton Boutique. The something may be a card case, a tennis racquet
cover, an ashtray or even an eyeglass case; Saks has thought of
everything.

Lingerie and Robes

Every woman has her own special loves, hates and requirements when it comes to lingerie, nightgowns and robes. Some
like them hot, some like them cool; some like them long, some
like them short; some like them diaphanous, others opaque;
some require natural fibers and others want them drip-dry.
Every department store has an extensive lingerie section, but
we've listed the few that we like best.

*ELIZABETH ARDEN / 691 Fifth Avenue between 54th and 55th
Streets / Monday through Saturday 9:00 to 5:30 / 486–7900*

At Arden's an entire half of the second floor is devoted to lingerie. It's
the home of the quilted bathrobe with matching nightgown.

*HENRI BENDEL / 10 West 57th Street between Fifth and Sixth
Avenues / Monday through Saturday, 10:00 to 5:30 / 247–1110*

Like all the merchandise at Bendel's, its nightgowns, sleeping pajamas,
and robes are made for the trendy, body-conscious lady.

*BERGDORF GOODMAN / 754 Fifth Avenue at 58th Street
Monday through Saturday 10:00 to 6:00, Thursday 10:00 to 8:00
753–7300*

The second-floor Lingerie Shop stocks light- and heavy-weight robes,
short and long nightgowns, winter and summer bed jackets, all made up
in the same exclusive Bergdorf pattern. There are also slips and panties
and Berlé brassieres.

*LERON / 745 Fifth Avenue between 57th and 58th Streets / Monday
through Friday 9:30 to 6:00, Saturday 9:30 to 5:00 / 753–6700*

When you enter these portals be prepared to forget any consideration of
cost. Leron designs and carries its own beautiful nightgowns, robes and
slips, and will make them to order in any fabric, from drip-dry to pure
silk satin.

MONTENAPOLEONE / 789 Madison Avenue between 66th and 67th Streets / Monday through Saturday 10:00 to 6:00 / 535-2660

This shop has slips, bras, bikinis, nightgowns and robes in cotton, silk and synthetic materials. You may buy from stock, or they will make any item to order. Their fabulous lingerie comes in every color of the rainbow, with liberal trimmings of lace.

NEW YORK EXCHANGE FOR WOMEN'S WORK 541 Madison Avenue between 54th and 55th Streets / Monday through Friday 9:30 to 5:00, Saturday 10:00 to 4:00 / 753-2330

The Women's Exchange is one of the few places one can find good warm handknit or crocheted bed jackets. Some are lined in silk.

D. PORTHAULT / 57 East 57th Street between Madison and Park Avenues / Monday through Friday 9:30 to 5:45, Saturday 9:30 to 4:45 / 688-1660

Terry cloth robes, long and short, cardigan or wrap, for women and men (and now even for infants), can be found here in the famous Porthault designs.

SAKS FIFTH AVENUE / 611 Fifth Avenue between 49th and 50th Streets / Monday through Saturday 10:00 to 6:00, Thursday 10:00 to 8:30 / 753-4000

Saks has a huge selection of robes, nightgowns, slips, and bras made in every color, size and fabric, with prices to suit the taste of every age group.

Liquors

See page 216.

Luggage

See page 117.

Maternity Clothes

Several department stores carry maternity clothes, including Bloomingdale's, Lord & Taylor and Saks Fifth Avenue. There are also a few specialty stores that cater to the needs of the *enceinte*.

LADY MADONNA / 793 Madison Avenue at 67th Street / Monday through Saturday 10:00 to 6:00, Thursday 10:30 to 8:30 / 988-7173

Good-looking maternity clothes are admittedly hard to find, but "Lady Madonnas" of all sizes can buy pretty, practical, wearable clothes for just about any occasion, be it in the morning, at noon or night. Prices permit you to throw these outsized garments away or pass them along to friends, without guilt, after the great event.

MATER'S MARKET / 237 East 53rd Street between Second and Third Avenues / Monday through Saturday 10:30 to 5:30, Tuesday 10:30 to 7:00 / 355-7977

This little maternity shop, five steps up from street level in a gaily painted old building, has a variety of clothing, including maternity jeans. They also have tiny T-shirts for the future arrival. All at very modest prices.

TENNIS LADY, INC. / 765 Madison Avenue between 65th and 66th Streets / Monday through Friday 10:00 to 6:00, Saturday 10:00 to 5:30 / 535-8601

If you are pregnant and still playing tennis, you can get maternity tennis clothes at Tennis Lady.

Men's Clothing

Men's fashion has changed dramatically in the last few years; now a man requires just as much closet and drawer space for his seasonal wardrobe as a woman does, and it takes him just as much thought, time and planning to get dressed. Men who can't cope with this new trend often prevail upon women to help them assemble their increasingly complicated ensembles. The best-dressed men we know rely on the shops listed below for their furnishings. Bergdorf Goodman, Bloomingdale's, Bonwit Teller and Saks Fifth Avenue also carry first-rate highly styled men's wear. Without exception, women are welcome in these emporiums either to buy the clothes for their men or to contribute their two-cents-worth of advice. The largest concentration of men's furnishing stores is on Madison Avenue beginning around 44th Street, though many fine shops are off the Avenue in the Fifties.

BARNEY'S / 111 Seventh Avenue at 17th Street / Monday through Saturday 9:00 A.M. to 9:30 P.M. / 929–9000

Barney's is a gigantic store with an enormous selection of designer clothes from around the world for men of all sizes and ages. It is a reasonably priced men's department store, although not a bargain center, that prides itself on not waiting on a customer until he's ready to be waited upon. In other words, they don't mind "just lookers."

BATTAGLIA SHOPS, INC. / 473 Park Avenue between 57th and 58th Streets / Monday through Friday 9:30 to 6:00, Saturday 9:30 to 5:15 / 755–1358

The Battaglia Shop is considered by many to be the finest men's store in the city. The Italian shoes, shirts, suits and other assorted haberdashery are highly priced and styled for the very thin and trendy male.

BROOKS BROTHERS / 346 Madison Avenue at 44th Street
Monday through Saturday 9:15 to 6:00 / 682–8800

The classic conservative Brooks Brothers look of the button-down collar and well-tailored suit is an old American tradition—and also traditional are the value and quality for your money. This men's department store takes care of the needs of the male from head to toe, be it boxer shorts, swimming trunks, sports shirts, raincoats, hats, lisle or wool socks, or even the very expensive Peal shoes. Their suits are sold "off the peg," but are fitted so beautifully they look bespoke.

DUNHILL TAILORED CLOTHES / 65 East 57th Street
between Madison and Park Avenues / Monday through Saturday
9:00 to 5:00 / 355–0050

Not to be confused with Dunhill pipes and cigars, Dunhill Tailored Clothes is an expensive men's haberdashery. It is famous for its distinctive blazers, which are available in every weight and color. Behind every fitting room door at Dunhill can be found a successful man having his final fitting on either a totally custom-made suit, a partially custom-made suit or one just taken from the peg. The difference in price depends upon whether they are made to measure, made in a standard size and then fitted, or whether only slight alterations are needed. The Brothers Block who own Dunhill know clothes and how to fit them to make every man's look successful.

R. MELEDANDRI, INC. / 74 East 56th Street between Madison
and Park Avenues / Monday through Saturday 9:30 to 6:00
753–1520

Meledandri is for taste-setters, not taste-followers. They have an array of beautiful fabrics for the customers who want clothes made to order. They also carry ready-to-wear sports clothes, great suits, resortwear and sweaters, shirts, ties and pocket handkerchiefs. Their things look expensive, and are.

PAUL STUART / Madison Avenue at 45th Street / Monday through
Saturday 9:00 to 6:00 / 682–0320

A two-story men's shop that carries suits, coats and haberdashery. Their forte with the men we know is the sheepskin coat, as well as turtleneck sweaters, leisure shirts and robes. Their suits seem to suit both the young and the old without undue strain on their wallets.

F. R. TRIPLER & COMPANY / Madison Avenue at 46th Street
Monday through Friday 9:00 to 5:45, Saturday 9:00 to 5:30
682–1760

Tripler's has an excellent selection of men's casual summer trousers in cotton plaids, stripes, checks and lots of solid colors. There you can also satisfy a "matchers" color palette in socks, bathing suits and even sweaters. Their suits, sports coats, etc., are on the upper floors, as are their hats (fur ones, too).

Museums

New York, New York has such a rich store of paintings, sculpture, artifacts, and other wonderous memorabilia stored in its museums that the casual visitor could never hope to see more than the "tip of the iceberg." If your stay here is limited, do make time for some of the permanent collections we've listed below. We're sure you'll be glad you did. The days and hours that museums are open are subject to change, so call before you set out. There are always special once-in-a-lifetime exhibits on display in these institutions, which you can ascertain by checking New York newspapers and magazines. For information about the Culture Buses that tour the museums, call 330–1234. Or you may write for a schedule (see p 133).

AMERICAN MUSEUM OF NATURAL HISTORY / Central
Park West at 79th Street / recorded announcement gives details of
activities and hours: 873–4225

There are thirty-seven permanent natural history exhibits here, including Animals and Birds of the World, Man in Africa, Eskimos, Minerals and Gems, Vertebrates, Ocean Life, Asian Mammals, and the Natural History of Central America, Mexico and North America.

THE CLOISTERS / Fort Tryon Park at 190th Street / Tuesday through Saturday 10:00 to 4:45, Sunday noon to 4:45 / 923-3700

A trip back into the Middle Ages awaits you at the Cloisters. In addition to several cloisters surrounding an inner garden, there is a replica of a medieval chapel. There are the world-renowned unicorn tapestries, a collection of priceless religious artifacts—and a setting that permits a spectacular view of the Hudson River. There are festivals in the spring and fall sponsored by the Metropolitan Museum.

COOPER-HEWITT MUSEUM / 2 East 91st Street between Fifth and Madison Avenues / Tuesday 10:00 to 9:00, Wednesday through Saturday 10:00 to 5:00, Sunday noon to 5:00 / 860-2011

The Cooper-Hewitt Museum is the Smithsonian Institution's National Museum for Design. The house itself is of great interest, having once been owned by Andrew Carnegie. The changing exhibits of blueprints, photographs and objects are concerned with Man and the designs he creates.

FRICK MUSEUM / 1 East 70th Street at Fifth Avenue / Tuesday through Saturday 10:00 to 6:00; Sunday 1:00 to 6:00 / 288-0700

European paintings, sculpture and decorative objects from the 14th to the 19th centuries are on exhibit in the Frick Museum. Once Henry Clay Frick's private mansion, it still reflects, with its arrangement of period furniture, flowers and tapestries, the handsome life style of its donor.

GUGGENHEIM MUSEUM / 1071 Fifth Avenue at 88th Street Tuesday 11:00 to 8:00; Wednesday through Sunday and holidays 11:00 to 5:00 / 860-1313

The Guggenheim Museum, one of Frank Lloyd Wright's last masterpieces, stands as a revolutionary approach to viewing art. Instead of separate galleries, it has a continuous spiraling ramp that leads the viewer from the bottom of the museum to the top (though most people elevator to the top and walk downhill). The Guggenheim's permanent collection consists of Impressionists, Post-Impressionists, contemporary paintings, drawings and sculpture. The museum has the largest collection of Kandinskys outside of Russia.

*HAYDEN PLANETARIUM / Central Park West at 81st Street
Monday through Friday 2:00 and 3:30, Saturday hourly from 11:00
to 5:00, Sunday hourly from 1:00 to 5:00 / 873–8828*

The planetarium consists of an inner dome auditorium where sky shows
can be seen from comfortable chairs. In addition, there are two
permanent displays: The Hall of the Sun, which shows the sun's
influence on our lives, and Astromedia, which is a potpourri of
astronomical data, fact and fancy. One of the most popular displays is
the Laserium, a light concert of laser beams shown on Friday, Saturday
and Sunday nights at 7:00, 8:30, 10:00 and 11:30.

*JEWISH MUSEUM / 1109 Fifth Avenue at 92nd Street / Monday
through Thursday noon to 5:00, Sunday 11:00 to 6:00 / 860–1888*

Historical memorabilia of the Jewish people are on permanent display:
the collection includes Judaic archeological artifacts, ritual objects, coins
and metals. From time to time special exhibits of contemporary art
works are shown.

*METROPOLITAN MUSEUM OF ART / Fifth Avenue at 82nd
Street / Tuesday 10:00 to 8:45, Wednesday through Saturday 10:00
to 4:45, Sunday 11:00 to 4:45 / 736–2211*

The Metropolitan permanent collection is encyclopedic. Some of the
highlights are Egyptian funerary objects, Islamic, Greek and Roman art,
ancient Near Eastern art, European decorative art, European period
rooms, Early American furnishings, art from the Middle Ages, the gallery
of arms and armor, and the Lehman Collection, which consists of
20th-century paintings, a large revolving drawing collection and period
rooms filled with 14th- through 17th-century paintings, furniture and
decorative art.

*MUSEUM OF AMERICAN FOLK ART / 49 West 53rd Street
between Fifth and Sixth Avenues / Tuesday through Sunday 10:30
to 5:30 / 581–2474*

There are three or four exhibitions a year centered around different
aspects of American folk art.

*MUSEUM OF THE AMERICAN INDIAN / Broadway at
155th Street / Tuesday through Sunday 1:00 to 5:00 / 283–2420*

Art and artifacts of the Indians of the Western hemisphere.

*MUSEUM OF THE CITY OF NEW YORK / Fifth Avenue at
103rd Street / Tuesday through Saturday 10:00 to 5:00, Sunday
1:00 to 5:00 / 534–1672*

What this museum is all about is New York. The permanent exhibits are
18th- and 19th-century American silver and furniture; 19th-century fire
engines; Cityrama, a multi-media 17-minute show on the history of New
York City from 1524 to the present; plus toys, doll houses and dioramas
of rooms, period clothes and furniture.

*MUSEUM OF MODERN ART / 11 West 53rd Street between
Fifth and Sixth Avenues / Monday, Tuesday, Friday, Saturday,
Sunday 11:00 to 6:00, Thursday 11:00 to 9:00 / 956–6100*

In addition to whatever special exhibit is current, some pieces from the
museum's own collection of paintings, sculpture, drawings, design objects
and photographs of work done between 1880 and the present are always on
display. In the sculpture garden there are always examples of the work of
Rodin, Henry Moore, Eli Nadelman, Max Ernst and Miró, to name a few.

*NEW YORK HISTORICAL SOCIETY / 170 Central Park
West at 77th Street / Tuesday through Sunday 1:00 to 5:00,
Saturday 10:00 to 5:00 / 873–3400*

On permanent display are Hudson River School landscapes, Early
American portraits, costume figurines from the 17th to the 20th centuries,
glass paperweights, Colonial rooms and the James Audubon Gallery.

*SOUTH STREET SEAPORT MUSEUM / 16 Fulton Street
Museum: Thursday through Monday noon to 6:00; ships: Friday
through Sunday noon to 5:00 / 766–9020*

The many points of interest are the Model Ship Gallery with the history
of ship-building and model-making; the Printing Gallery with
19th-century American printing presses and a working print shop; an art
gallery of changing shows; a permanent bicentennial exhibition,
"Farewell to Old England"; a 309-foot four-masted bark called the
Peking, a former merchant vessel which can be explored on foot; a
market area with craft vendors; a nautical book and chart shop; and in
summer, daily harbor sails can be taken on a 1890 fishing schooner. Folk
song and dance are featured on the pier during the summer, as well as
many other special folk or craft exhibits.

WHITNEY MUSEUM / 924 Madison Avenue at 75th Street
Tuesday 11:00 to 10:00, Wednesday through Friday 11:00 to 6:00,
Saturday and Sunday noon to 6:00 / 794–0600

For forty-five years the Whitney has featured a biennial exhibition which surveys the current state of contemporary American art. In addition to contemporary masters, the biennials provide a showcase for a diverse group of lesser-known artists, some of whose works are bought for the museum's permanent collection.

Needlepoint

When Americans turned their thoughts and their hands to needlepoint, New York designers led a creative surge back to individualized canvases. Consequently, together with a huge selection of ready-to-make scrims, all the shops listed below will handpaint a design of your choice for eyeglass cases, pincushions, telephone book covers, luggage rack straps, coasters, slippers, handbags, belts, picture frames, chair covers, wall hangings and rugs of any size or shape, and furnish you with the colors of the finest wools with which to work. These shops also do expert finishing on the items bought from them—and charge accordingly.

ALICE MAYNARD / 133 East 65th Street between Lexington and
Park Avenues / Monday through Friday 10:00 to 6:00 / 535–6107

Alice Maynard has a large selection of needlepoint in stock, some commercial packages and some things designed just for them by free-lance artists. In-house artists also will create any item designed to your order. For the beginner, Maynard gives lessons; for the experts who want to design their own things, there is canvas by the yard. This shop also carries a good choice of yarns for needlepoint, knitting, crocheting, embroidery and crewel work. If you require strands of yarn for special pieces, avoid Maynard's during the rush hours from 12 to 2.

*ROSE RIFF / 242 East 71st Street between Second and Third Avenues
Monday through Friday 9:00 to 6:00, Saturday 9:00 to 5:00
628–8823*

Once you've completed the stitches of any needlepoint item (except slippers), Rose Riff will bind, block, line or do whatever else is necessary to finish it off. And generally her services are less than the "on the Avenue" shops.

*ERICA WILSON NEEDLE WORKS / 717 Madison Avenue
between 63rd and 64th Streets / Monday through Friday 9:30 to
5:30, Saturday 10:00 to 5:00 / closed Saturdays in the summer
832–7290*

Once this second-floor shop specialized in crewel work, but today Erica Wilson devotes equal attention to needlepoint. A good selection of original designs.

*WOOL FARM / 49 East 10th Street between University Place and
Broadway / Tuesday through Saturday 10:30 to 7:00 / 228–1760*

Not worth going out of the way for if you're only doing small things, but for larger needlepoint projects, such as rugs, wall hangings, etc., there is a huge selection of designs and wools at much lower prices than the midtown shops.

*WOOLWORKS, INC. / 838 Madison Avenue between 69th and
70th Streets / Monday through Friday 9:00 to 5:00 / 861–8700*

This attractive shop has its own stable of designers, who tend towards the modern. Bold designs, mostly on large-mesh canvases, are a specialty of the house, as is the originality of its smaller items.

Open on Sunday

There's a whole new thing going on in N.Y., N.Y. these days —more and more shops and department stores are staying open on Sunday. The advertisements in the local newspapers are the best guide to when and which department stores are following this trend. Here we've pooled our knowledge of other "Open on Sunday" places which cater to our minor emergencies, needs, wishes and wants. More specific information about each place listed below can be found under its general category. (For example, see Restaurants, Antique Dealers, etc.)

ANTIQUE DEALERS

ANTIQUE CENTER OF AMERICA / 415 East 53rd Street
between First Avenue and Sutton Place / noon to 6:00 / 486–0941

MANHATTAN ART AND ANTIQUES CENTER / 1050
Second Avenue between 55th and 56th Streets / noon to 6:00
355–4400

BEAUTY

LARRY MATTHEWS / 45 East 55th Street at Madison Avenue
9:00 to 5:00 / 246–6100

BOOKS

BRENTANO'S / 26 University Place at 8th Street / 12:30 to 7:30
674-3480

DRUG STORES

EDWARD'S DRUG STORE / 225 East 57th Street between
Second and Third Avenues / 10:00 to 5:00 / 753-2830;
prescription department: 753-2885

KAUFMAN PHARMACY / Lexington Avenue at 50th Street / never
closes / 755-2266

FLORISTS

TERRESTRIS / 409 East 60th Street between First and York Avenues
8:00 A.M. to 11:00 P.M. / 758-8181

FURNITURE

W. J. SLOANE, INC. / Fifth Avenue at 38th Street / noon to 5:00
695-3800

GIFTS PERSONALIZED

T-Shirts

P & J STATIONERY / 882 First Avenue at 50th Street / 7:00 A.M.
to 2:00 P.M. / 755-1988

HAYRIDES

CHATEAU STABLES, INC. / 608 West 48th Street between Eleventh and Twelfth Avenues / 8:00 to 6:00 / 246–0520

KITCHEN AND HOUSEWARES

POTTERY BARN / 117 East 59th Street between Lexington and Park Avenues / noon to 5:00 / 838–7130

MUSEUMS

All New York museums are open on Sunday (see page 125 for some of our favorites). A "Culture Bus" travels from one museum to another on Saturdays and Sundays for a cost of $1.25. Information on schedules can be obtained from the Transit Authority Information Booths in Grand Central Station and Pennsylvania Station, or by calling the New York City Transit Authority at 330–1234. You can write for a copy of the Culture Bus schedule to: Bus Maps, New York City Transit Authority, 25 Jamaica Avenue, Brooklyn, New York 11207. Include a self-addressed stamped envelope and be prepared to wait about a month for a reply.

PARTY FOOD

Caviar and . . .

CAVIARTERIA / 870 Madison Avenue between 70th and 71st Streets 9:00 to 6:00 / closed Sunday July and August / 861–1210

LA FONTANELLA / 1304 Second Avenue between 68th and 69th Streets / 2:00 to 7:00 / 988–4778

Delicatessens

DOVER DELICACIES / *144 East 57th Street between Lexington and Third Avenues* / *8:00 AM to 11:00 P.M.* / *delivers* / *759–2570*

SBARRO GOURMET / *1245 Second Avenue between 65th and 66th Streets* / *9:00 A.M. to 10:00 P.M.* / *752–9837*

STAGE DELICATESSEN AND RESTAURANT
834 Seventh Avenue between 53rd and 54th Streets / *never closes*
245–7850

Desserts

CAKE MASTERS / *1111 Third Avenue at 65th Street* / *8:00 A.M. to 8:30 P.M.* / *759–7212*

Fruit and Vegetables

PERRONE'S / *1120 Third Avenue between 65th and 66th Streets*
10:00 to 6:00 / *249–3950; 535–0335*

Ice

CIRCLE ICE COMPANY / *733 Ninth Avenue between 37th and 38th Streets* / *9:00 to 9:00* / *873–7469*

RECORD SHOPS

COLONY RECORDS / *1671 Broadway at 49th Street / 9:30* A.M. *to 2:30* A.M. */ 265–2050*

KING KAROL RECORDS / *126 West 42nd Street between Sixth Avenue and Broadway / 11:00 to 8:00 / 354–6880*

SAM GOODY / *1290 Sixth Avenue at 51st Street / noon to 5:00 246–8730*

RESTAURANTS

See pages 183–84.

Party Provisions

N.Y., N.Y. is a party town. New Yorkers go to a lot of them and give a lot of them. Some parties are business-oriented, some are for fund-raising, and others are for just plain old fun-raising.

Fortunately, in our town all kinds of services exist to help simplify party-giving. For example, equipment (tables, chairs, coat racks, flatware, tablecloths, napkins, serving dishes, trays, china, glasses, chafing dishes, candlesticks and serving pieces) can be had on a straight rental basis, or a caterer will supply all of the above and food, too (as well as someone to serve it). Or you can prepare and/or buy food ready-cooked; and/or buy part of the menu and have the rest catered. Get the idea? New York gives you lots of options for giving a party. Get them in one package, mix them or match them.

CATERERS

They come. They cook. They serve. They clean up and go away. There are caterers in New York who are equipped to serve a dinner for a cast of thousands with ease, and others who get as nervous as the hostess if there are more than 40 guests. Obviously, quality has to be somewhat sacrificed for quantity, but even a marvelous caterer's chef can have his off nights. Dealing with caterers is like being an ion in a magnetic field: it can be a negative or positive experience. Since costs are generally figured by the head, it's who works best for you that counts. A good caterer will help you select a menu that's feasible in the space, time and equipment available *in situ*.

ROBERT DAY DEAN'S / 36–56 34th Street, Long Island City
Monday through Friday 9:00 to 4:30 / 755–8300

Robert Day Dean is one of the deans of New York catering and without him many a charity ball could never have bounced. He will do the traditional menu from soup to nuts with beef or chicken in between. Not only will he provide the food for cocktails, luncheon, dinner or late supper, he can supply the waiters and waitresses to serve it, tables and appropriate napery and silver, and even gilt ballroom chairs for your guests to sit on. His prices, like the fare, run from reasonable to elaborate.

GLORIOUS FOODS, INC. / 172 East 75th Street between Lexington and Third Avenues / 628-2320

When people get bored with the same food and table settings, they are apt to go to a new caterer instead of asking their old one to think up something new. And Glorious Food represents the new wave of mass feeding. Typical of their concept of elegance is the presentation for hors d'oeuvres of cold raw vegetables (crudités) arranged like a bouquet of flowers in a basket, or clams and oysters served on a bed of ice and garnished with seaweed instead of parsley. Their main courses are fairly typical and so are their desserts—except for the manner in which they are served. (Strawberries, for instance, arrive in a tall-stemmed glass.) They cater to a minimum of 18 people. They say only a couple of days' notice is needed, but you should book well in advance for they are quite busy. They will arrange rentals of tables and table settings for you.

JOSEPH MILLER / 315 East 65th Street between First and Second Avenues / answering service will take messages 24 hours a day: 861-7923

Mr. Miller's forte is buffet dinners, where he presents seven or eight different delicious hors d'oeuvres, an equal number of fantastic dessert choices and a nice variety of what goes in between. Everything is in good taste and everything tastes good. His waiters are beautifully aware of guests' wants and the boss is usually there to supervise. He charges by the head and doesn't like to cater to less than fifty persons. He's less busy, and therefore more apt to be available on short notice, in January, February and March. Other times, plan well ahead if you want Mr. Miller in person. He will arrange to rent napery, etc., if you need it.

RESTAURANT ASSOCIATES / 1540 Broadway / Monday through Friday 10:00 to 5:00 / 974-6700

If you think big, they are the people for you. Restaurant Associates will cater to a minimum of 150 people; the most we know they've fed is 2,000. For enormous crowds, such as an inaugural ball, they need a month's notice. Their concept of food is always original, but if you want to stay on the beaten path they can do that too. Their unique specialty is a huge buffet in an outdoor or enclosed space. Even when dealing in large numbers, the food is good and well presented.

*RUDOLPH STANISH / 130 East 67th Street between Lexington
and Park Avenues / answering service will take messages:
355–0110*

Rudolph Stanish travels from party to party to party, from New York to
California, from Maine to Florida. This remarkable one-man show makes
omelettes of fine herbs, cheese, bacon and jambon as fast as guests can
order and eat them. His omelettes and a salad are the mainstay of
breakfast, lunch and late-night parties. Because he is an "original," you
have to book him well in advance. He makes omelettes before the eyes
of 2 or 200 guests and has an assistant who dishes out salad or sweet
rolls (depending on the time of day, or your wishes). Mr. Stanish keeps
everyone happy and coming back for more.

*DONALD BRUCE WHITE / 159 East 64th Street between
Lexington and Third Avenues / Monday through Friday 10:00 to
5:00, Saturday 1:00 to 5:00 / 988–8410*

Donald Bruce White has very good recipes and a superb chef, and,
moreover, is willing to take your family recipe and make it work for a
large number of people. He likes the idea of serving different yet good
food and is interested in working with someone who feels the same way
about it. Like all true artists, he can be temperamental, but an artist is
an artist is an artist. If it's superb food you're after, he is at his best with
numbers ranging from 12 people to several dozen, but he can and has
served 400 or 500. For larger parties Donald will rent equipment for you
from the usual sources.

*CHARLES WILSON, LTD. / 22 East 66th Street between Fifth
and Madison Avenues / Monday through Friday 9:30 to 4:30; also
has answering service / 879–6020*

One call does *all* at Wilson's. Their firm name is Ltd., but they are not.
They will do a party for you for 10 guests or 1,000, and do everything
from producing food to supplying maitre d's, bartenders, bars, dance
floors and/or tents. They need a week to two weeks' notice if you are
thinking *big*. Also see page 139.

PARTY EQUIPMENT

If you want to do the food yourself and need something to put it on, or something to put your guests at, or what have you, these are the places we call.

ROBERT DAY DEAN'S / 36–56 34th Street, Long Island City
Monday through Friday 9:00 to 4:30 / 755–8300

Rental of basic party equipment is just one of their services. For tables and chairs and other such, they need two to three days' notice for delivery. If it's catering the whole number, from soup to soufflé, they need at least two weeks' notice. This is a well-established institution in N.Y., and very reliable. Also see page 136.

SERVICE PARTY- RENTAL / 521 East 72nd Street between
York Avenue and the East River / Monday through Friday 9:00 to
5:30 / 288–7384

One of the advantages of Service Party Rentals is that it is located on the East Side of Manhattan. This means you can look before you rent— at dishes, flatware, wine coolers, tables, chairs and whichever and whatever you would, and if it's at the zero hour you can even get it to your place in a taxi. Although there is no minimum charge for cash-and-carry rentals, you must spend $30 before they will deliver.

CHARLES WILSON, LTD. / 22 East 66th Street between Fifth
and Madison Avenues / Monday through Friday 9:30 to 4:30; also
has answering service / 879–6020

This old establishment caterer also has tables, ballroom chairs and complete dinner services to rent. Wilson's items are often reproductions of N.Y.'s finest families' real things, and the Wilson staff is very nice.

Also see: Hayrides, page 164.

PARTY FAVORS

The time-honored party favors for children and grown-ups are available in department stores and five-and-tens, but in N.Y., N.Y. we also have specialty shops that are solely devoted to party goods.

MARY ARNOLD / 965 Lexington Avenue at 70th Street / Monday through Friday 9:00 to 6:00, Saturday 10:00 to 6:00 / 744–8510

The ultimate provider of supplies for children's parties, from the paper napkins to balloons, assorted prizes, gifts, place cards, invitations, and, if you get desperate, they even know some magicians. Their ample stock allows you to decide if you want to give a party for pennies or go for broke.

HALLMARK GALLERY / 720 Fifth Avenue at 56th Street Monday through Saturday 9:30 to 6:30 / 489–8320

Everything in paper you need for a party from the invitations, decorations and gift wrappings to the thank-you cards.

PAPER HOUSE / 741 Madison Avenue between 64th and 65th Streets / Monday through Saturday 9:30 to 6:30 / 737–0082

Paper House has decorative favors, centerpieces, garlands, toys, balloons, shower and wedding supplies, cards . . . in fact, everything but the party.

PARTY BAZAAR / 390 Fifth Avenue at 36th Street / Monday 8:00 to 7:00, Tuesday, Wednesday, Friday, Saturday 8:00 to 6:00, Thursday 8:00 to 8:00 / 695–6820

Featuring Dennison's world famous products, Party Bazaar has a plethora of party goods, for big people and for little people, whether it's to honor the christening of a newborn or a ship, a wedding or a golden anniversary, or a birthday—yours or George Washington's. In addition, they have clear plastic glasses (in wine, old-fashioned and highball sizes) which not only can be recycled, but even monogrammed!

TOY BALLOON CORP. / 204 East 38th Street between Second and Third Avenues / Monday through Friday 9:00 to 5:00 682–3803

This unique shop will imprint balloons of all sizes, shapes and colors in any quantity. If your order is small they'll do it while you wait. If you're covering an entire ballroom ceiling with balloons saying, "I'm just wild about Harry," or any other appropriate phrase or name, you have to give them some advance notice. They'll inflate the balloons for you in their shop or at the party, at not-too-inflated prices.

PARTY FOOD

Even without culinary ability or elaborate cooking facilities you can serve a gourmet breakfast, lunch, tea, dinner or supper in a home, a hotel room or an office in New York. You can buy some or all of any meal from the excellent purveyors we've listed below.

Breads, Desserts and . . .

BLOOMINGDALE'S BREAD DEPARTMENT / Lexington Avenue between 59th and 60th Streets / Monday and Thursday 9:45 to 9:00, Tuesday, Wednesday, Friday, Saturday 9:45 to 6:00 355–5900

A diet of bread and water could be acceptable and even delicious if the bread came from Bloomingdale's. From bagel to brioche, from Irish to Italian, from sourdough to Syrian, from a small single roll shaped like a turtle to a long alligator loaf, the choice is endless. Bloomie's bread is usually baked daily.

Beyond Bloomingdale's bread counter is a gourmet grocery shop and, to one side, there is an excellent cheese shop.

BONTÉ PATISSERIE / 1316 Third Avenue between 75th and 76th Streets / Monday through Saturday 9:00 to 7:00 / 535–2360

This bakery produces the prettiest birthday cakes in town, and maybe the richest and most delicious. Their decorations are pure art—a rose and the name of the celebratee, beautifully scripted, are just two of the specialties of this *patisserie*. They also have fabulous tarts, pastries, and quiches. It's a small place, but if you get unexpectedly stuck, they produce a cake in a hurry.

CAKE MASTERS / 1111 Third Avenue at 65th Street / Monday through Saturday 8:00 A.M. to 10:00 P.M., Sunday 8:00 A.M. to 8:30 P.M. / 759–7212

These "Masters" make all kinds of cakes, to commemorate all sorts of occasions. In addition, they have plain old sweet breakfast rolls and cookies.

COLETTE / 1136 Third Avenue between 66th and 67th Streets Tuesday through Saturday 9:00 to 6:00 / 988–2605

Colette is justly renowned for her large, fresh-from-the-oven brioches, croissants, quiche Lorraine, French pastries and chocolate cake. She will also prepare boeuf bourguignon, veal blanquette and coq au vin for any number of people. Nearly everything is on hand, but to be sure, it's safer to order in advance.

CREATIVE CAKES / 400 East 74th Street at First Avenue Tuesday through Friday 10:00 to 5:00, Saturday 11:00 to 2:00 794–9811

Stephanie at Creative Cakes makes cakes to look like people's faces or their favorite houses, books, pets, food or cars. The cake is baked into its shape, iced in Technicolor detail to strengthen the resemblance, and then further adorned with a name, title or saying. To order a Creative Cake, supply a photograph, preferably in color, of the subject you want "caked." Give Stephanie about a week's advance notice because she's so busy. Her smallest cake is $35 and as the size gets larger, the price gets higher.

DUMAS PATISSERIE / 116 East 60th Street between Lexington and Park Avenues / Monday and Thursday 10:00 to 8:00, Tuesday, Wednesday, Friday, Saturday 10:00 to 7:00 / 688–0905

Fabulous, flaky croissants are made hourly at Dumas. This is a true French patisserie, in the most delicious sense of the word. The air is redolent with the tantalizing smells of croissants, pastries and every conceivable kind of cookies emerging hot from the ovens. Dumas also carries imported cheeses.

WILLIAM GREENBERG, JR. BAKERY / 817 Madison
Avenue at 68th Street / Monday through Saturday 9:30 to 6:00
535–7118
   1377 Third Avenue between 78th and 79th Streets / Monday
through Saturday 9:30 to 6:00 / 876–2255

William Greenberg, Jr. is a person who minds his own store (the one on
Third Avenue). It is only there that you can get his personally decorated
chocolate cakes, be they for birthdays, weddings or whatever. Both of his
shops have some of the best cookies and honey buns that non-calorie-
counters could hope for.

MRS. HERBST / 1437 Third Avenue at 81st Street / Monday through
Saturday 8:00 to 6:30 / 535–8484

Mrs. Herbst makes the best apple, cheese, cherry, nut, poppy seed and
cabbage strudel this side of Budapest. Also hard to resist are her coffee
rings, cookies and Danish pastry. Not only will she mail her cakes
(providing it's only a few hundred miles), but on occasion she can be
persuaded to put an order on a Greyhound bus to be picked up hours
later. Orders over $8 will be delivered.

LEONARD BAKING CO. / Third Avenue at 80th Street / Monday
through Friday 9:00 to 5:00, Saturday 9:00 to 4:00 / 734–2300

If you are a nut for coconut layer cake, this is the bakery for you. Other
specialties are chocolate or strawberry mousse cake and a divine orange
sponge. Nor is their cheese cake the worst thing you ever put in your
mouth. With a day or two advance notice they will deliver.

Caviar and . . .

The fanciest of fancy foods is unquestionably caviar—and some caviar is
fancier than others, though all of it is expensive. When you buy it in a jar
at the neighborhood grocer, it's salted for preservation—and if its price
makes you feel faint, the price of "fresh" caviar will give you cardiac arrest.
If you are out to make an investment in caviar, know this: the choicest and
therefore the most expensive of this sturgeon roe is labeled Fresh Beluga
"3–0." Needless to say, N.Y. has excellent purveyors of fresh caviar, be it
Russian or Iranian you are after. Russian comes from one side of the Black
Sea and Iranian from the other; the quality is the same. The price difference
in America between the two is based on import duty.
   There are many other party foods available in our town—some imported,
some home-grown.

*BRUNCHERIA LUNCHEONETTE / 25 West 58th Street
between Fifth and Sixth Avenues / Monday through Friday 6:00
A.M. to 7:00 P.M., Saturday 10:00 to 4:00 / 753–6780*

For luncheon or cocktail fare, if you're feeling Italian, Bruncheria makes darn good pizzas. They come in one size only so you can eat the whole thing yourself or divide it up into eight slices. The little old pizza maker starts making at 10:00 and closes shop at 6:00. They'll deliver uptown and downtown "provided it's a good order." Question: "What's a good order?" Answer: "A pizza!"

*CAVIARTERIA / 870 Madison Avenue between 70th and 71st Streets
Monday through Sunday 9:00 to 6:00 / closed Sunday July and
August / 861–1210*

The specialty at Caviarteria is—you guessed it—caviar, though they do have other delicacies. When last priced their fresh Iranian Beluga caviar was about the same as everyone else's, which is to say it was approximately $10 an ounce. The smaller-egged Sevruga costs slightly more than $6 an ounce.

*CHARLES & CO. / 683 Madison Avenue between 62nd and 63rd
Streets / Monday through Saturday 8:00 to 6:00 / 832–9430*

Fresh caviar is sold here in 3 1/2-ounce jars, but larger quantities are also available. This fancy grocer has lots of English biscuits, tea, out-of-season fruit, cheese, and gift baskets and boxes filled with fruits, jams, candies and even steaks. These gifts are available already made up or filled to your order. At holiday time Charles & Co. carries gingerbread houses for decking your home, halls or table.

*FRASER-MORRIS / 872 Madison Avenue between 70th and 71st
Streets / Monday through Saturday 9:00 to 6:00 / 988–6700*

Fraser-Morris carries price-is-no-object food treats from all over the world. They stock caviar from Iran, salmon from Scotland and Ireland, pompidons from India, cheeses from France and Italy, pâté de foie gras and mustard (Fauchon) from France, tea and candy from England and fresh fruits from New Zealand. And their pumpernickel bread made right here in New York is a worthy companion to all of their delicacies. They routinely deliver in Manhattan and have a special service for as far away as Connecticut.

LA FONTANELLA / 1304 Second Avenue between 68th and 69th Streets / Monday through Saturday 11:00 to 8:00, Sunday 2:00 to 7:00 / 988–4778

Excellent quiche and super-rich chocolate cake are good things to order from La Fontanella.

MAISON GLASS / 52 East 58th Street between Madison and Park Avenues / Monday through Saturday 8:45 to 5:45 / 755–3316

Maison Glass is a gourmet's delight of delicious imported delicacies. In addition to fresh Iranian caviar, the specialties of the house are fresh-roasted nuts (2 1/2 pounds of macadamias, pecans, cashews and hazelnuts for $17.50), seasonings, soups, pâtés, Bar-Le-Duc, jellies, jams, quiche Lorraine, canned snails, potted shrimp, canned meats and candies. They even carry a small assortment of gourmet cooking dishes. Everything is so attractively packaged it can serve as an instant gift.

MANGANARO'S HERO BOY RESTAURANT / 492 Ninth Avenue between 37th and 38th Streets / Monday through Saturday 6:00 a.m. to 7:30 p.m. / 947–7325

If you like to share sandwiches, Manganaro's makes one you can divide among at least 40 people. It's a six-foot-long, seven-inch-wide loaf of Italian bread split down the center and chockfull of layers and layers of beef, ham, salami, cheese, lettuce, tomato and Italian spices. For the nonpurist they'll substitute roast beef and/or turkey. All this goodness goes by many names: a submarine, a grinder, a hoagy, an Italian sandwich, but to us and Manganaro's it's a *hero*. Order heros by the foot and figure it by the number you want to feed: 2 feet long feeds 10 people; 4 feet long feeds 20 people; 6 feet long feeds 40 people. The cost is about $10 per foot, which includes the board it rests on and a sharp cutting knife.

WILLIAM POLL / 1051 Lexington Avenue between 75th and 76th Streets / Monday through Saturday 9:00 to 6:00 / 288–0501

William Poll's is not only a place to buy fresh Iranian caviar, it is also a super delicatessen that will prepare trays of hors d'oeuvres, dips and pâté for parties of any size or occasion. For tailgating picnics, or lunch at the executive desk, Poll's sandwiches have no equal.

Delicatessens

DOVER DELICACIES / 144 East 57th Street between Lexington and Third Avenues / Monday through Saturday 7:00 A.M. to 1:30 A.M., Sunday 8:00 A.M. to 11:00 P.M. / 759–2570

Here you can go in and buy a single sandwich, a tray (yours or theirs) of assorted cold meats, Nova Scotia salmon, plain lox, cheeses, breads (including bagels), fruits and vegetables, canned and packaged groceries. For Jewish holidays you can order traditional dishes, from matzoh to gefilte fish, challah and freshly ground horseradish. They'll take large and small orders by phone, and will deliver at the time they say they will.

SBARRO GOURMET / 1245 Second Avenue between 65th and 66th Streets / Monday through Sunday 9:00 A.M. to 10:00 P.M. 752–9837

Sbarro Gourmet has all the salads, meats, cheeses, peppers and packaged goods anyone would want for a good Italian dinner. They always have freshly cooked hot dishes on hand, and will also cook up others to special order. Among the mouth-watering specialities are their own stuffed sausages and all kinds of crusty Italian bread. You can go to the shop or order by phone. In either case they will deliver.

STAGE DELICATESSEN AND RESTAURANT / 834 Seventh Avenue between 53rd and 54th Streets / never closes 245–7850

Heartburn Heaven! Hot pastrami and corned beef (made as they were in the Old Countries) make the Stage a must stop for delicatessen devotees. You can eat on the premises, or they will deliver their goodies to you. Some of their other treats are knockwurst, liverwurst, garlic pickles, cole slaw, sauerkraut and fresh-fresh rye bread.

Fish, Groceries, Meat and Produce

GRISTEDE'S / 55 East 59th Street between Madison and Park
Avenues / Monday through Saturday 8:00 to 6:00 / 758–2460

A large, self-service store, with a smattering of all household goods and groceries, and a counter with cooked foods. They do not sell their goods at supermarket prices, but they do deliver and will open charge accounts.

LEONARD'S FISH MARKET / 1213 Third Avenue at 70th Street
Monday through Friday 8:00 to 6:00, Saturday 8:00 to 4:00
744–2600; 288–3390

Whether you want your fish fresh, smoked or frozen, Leonard has it. They'll shuck, shell, bone, or poach it if you so desire, and whether your fancy turns to shrimps for hors d'oeuvres or soft-shell crabs, Dover sole or smoked trout, this is your place. They also carry gourmet cuts of meat and know how to butcher them correctly. Quality is their concern, even in their delivery service.

J. OTTOMANELLI & SONS MEAT MARKET / 1155 First
Avenue at 63rd Street / Monday through Friday 7:00 to 6:00,
Saturday 7:00 to 4:00 / 355–4413

Prime cuts of all the usual meats, plus fresh game when it's in season—plump partridge, perfect pheasant, great grouse, quail, rabbit and others, too. Just ask for Frank. They deliver.

PERRONE'S / 1120 Third Avenue between 65th and 66th Streets
Monday through Saturday 8:00 A.M. to 9:00 P.M., Sunday 10:00 to
6:00 / 249–3950; 535–0335

If a recipe or your taste buds suddenly require an out-of-season fresh fruit or vegetable, rush to Perrone's. (Of course they have in-season produce, too.) All of it is beautifully displayed and if you don't see it, ask for it. This fresh beauty costs money, and if you have any left you can enjoy a glass of freshly squeezed orange juice while they bag your purchases. If you buy enough they'll deliver.

PISACANE / 940 First Avenue between 51st and 52nd Streets
Monday through Saturday 8:00 to 5:00 / 752–7560

Here is an authentic sawdust-on-the-floor fish market where freshness and variety of the fish and crustaceans are the raison d'etre. Piscane will open charge accounts and has same-day delivery service. Love it.

Hors D'Oeuvres

NYBORG & NELSON / 937 Second Avenue between 49th and 50th Streets / Monday through Saturday 10:00 to 7:00 / 355-9141

The makings of an entire Swedish smörgåsbord are always available at Nyborg & Nelson. The ready-to-take-home delicacies include pickled herring, liver pâté with cucumber sauce, meat balls, crab or shrimp salad, and the wonderful, wonderful cured salmon called "gravlax," which they serve with dill sauce. And all this at reasonable prices, which makes giving a cocktail buffet easy—providing you have your own aquavit.

OLD DENMARK / 133 East 65th Street between Lexington and Third Avenues / Monday through Saturday 9:00 to 6:00 744-2533

One of the ways to find your favorites is to go in hungry and start tasting. You can buy a whole plateful of samplings at a reasonable price. Some taste treats they offer are salads, pâtés, dips, crackers, breads, candies and heavenly Danish smoked salmon. The latter you can buy by the piece, pound or side, depending on how rich you feel.

TINO VASQUEZ / 124 East 85th Street between Lexington and Park Avenues / call in advance: 988-2985

Mr. Vasquez makes delicious hors d'oeuvres of unusual combinations in his tiny immaculate kitchen. Orders must be placed in advance and by phone. You tell Mr. Vasquez how many hors d'oeuvres you want and he makes a variety of finger food, the ingredients for which depend upon his whim. No deliveries, and if you are afraid of cats, have a friend pick up your order.

. . . And Who Can Have A Party Without Ice

CIRCLE ICE & CUBE COMPANY / 733 Ninth Avenue / daily 9:00 A.M. to 9:00 P.M. / 873-7469

Circle Ice carries dry ice, blocks of ice and ice cubes, which they sell by the bag. They take orders by phone and will deliver, within the hour, as little as one bag. Besides all this service they create ice statues such as a 4-foot standing sturgeon to use as a receptacle for fresh caviar, or any other ice sculpture you can dream up. Ice sculpture prices start at $75.

EMPIRE ICE CUBE COMPANY / 434 West 38th Street
daily / 594-5212

If you are a good customer and desperate, Empire will try to deliver ice to you within a half hour. (Time, of course, depends upon how far away you are from them.) In addition to ice cubes and ice blocks, they also sell ice shaved and chopped.

PARTY MUSIC

The price of live music in New York depends upon who is leading the band, how many pieces are in it and how many hours they are booked to play. (Prices begin at union scale, which is about $100 per man for continuous playing for 3 1/2 to 4 hours.) Certain party rooms in large hotels require a minimum number of union musicians if live music is to be used; other rooms have no such requirements. The musicians we've listed below are ones we've used for all sorts of occasions. All of them are in great demand and, therefore, it's best to try to book them well in advance.

MICHAEL CARNEY ORCHESTRA / 200 East 71st Street /
628-4447

The leader of this band, Mike Carney, has got plenty of personality and his music is like him: young, lively and fun. He himself plays the piano for smaller parties, but be sure to book well in advance.

RAY COHEN; JERRY KRAVAT ENTERTAINMENT
SERVICES / 770 Lexington Avenue / 758-3333

Ray Cohen at the piano is the special ingredient that ensures a party ending up in an old-fashioned nostalgic songfest.

BEN CUTLER / 21 Crows Neck Road, Bronxville, New York
914-779-8602

Ben Cutler and his group concentrate on Cole Porter and Rodgers-Hammerstein favorites. However, he can provide rock groups, or any other type of combo your party requires.

PETER DUCHIN ORCHESTRAS, INC. / 400 Madison Avenue
   753-4393

Through Peter Duchin you can hire individual piano players, guitarists, accordionists, trios, rock groups (live or taped) and big or little bands. For a large fee, Peter himself will sit at the piano and happily tickle the ivories. His personality makes every party a little more fun.

WILLIAM HARRINGTON / 516-627-0388

Bill Harrington at a piano is like having a whole dance band. You can also have a whole dance band along with Bill Harrington at the piano.

BERT KENT / Overlook Road, Ossining, New York / 914-762-0520

Bert Kent is a man for all seasons, all occasions and all instruments (that is, the guitar, banjo and accordion). He sings, he's a strolling musician, he's a leader of sing-along songs—in short, he's the life of any party. He'll bring other musicians along with him, if you want a bigger sound.

LESTER LANIN / 157 West 57th Street / 265-5208

One of the all-time popular society dance bands, Lester Lanin's orchestra plays for debutante parties, proms, weddings and private parties. He will also supply strolling musicians and guitarists. For an extra fee, the maestro himself will lead the band.

FORREST G. PERRIN / 162 West 54th Street / 245-7690

Many, in fact most, New York fashion models have danced, waltzed, tangoed, rocked or hustled down the runway to the beat of Forrest's combos. He knows all the current tunes, plus lots of golden oldies. You can book Forrest singly to play the piano for a little background music, with a small three- or four-piece combo or with his entire orchestra. He also has a library of taped music and will set up and run an instant discotheque for you.

PARTY ROOMS

You can give a party almost anywhere in New York: in a home, in an office, or if you want to think big, in a restaurant, museum, an art gallery, atop a building, on a ferry that circles Manhattan, on an ocean liner, in a department store, a zoo, a botanical garden or even, with permission of the proper city authorities, on an entire city block. If you are afraid of gambling on the elements, you can, again with permission, pitch a tent in an appropriate open space, such as the skating rink at Rockefeller Center or the lower plaza of the General Motors building.

More traditional places and spaces would include hotel ballrooms—small or grand. With the sponsorship of a member you can also rent a party place in many of New York's private clubs, such as Cosmopolitan, Colony, Doubles, El Morocco, Le Club, Metropolitan, New York Athletic Club, River Club and Union League Club, and most all of the university-affiliated clubs.

The rooms listed below require as much or as little effort as the host or hostess cares to contribute. With them, you have the special advantage of dining privately with your friends, as well as all the available services.

Hotel Ballrooms

AMERICANA HOTEL OF NEW YORK / Seventh Avenue between 52nd and 53rd Streets / 581–1000

Imperial Ballroom—capacity 3,200
Georgia Ballroom—capacity 850
Royal Ballroom—capacity 350
(The larger ballrooms can be subdivided)

ESSEX HOUSE / 160 Central Park South between Sixth and Seventh Avenues / 247–0300

Casino-on-the-Park Ballroom—capacity 500

NEW YORK HILTON HOTEL / Sixth Avenue between 53rd and 54th Streets / 586-7000

Grand Ballroom—capacity 3750 (can be divided into 2 rooms)
Sutton Ballroom—capacity 900 (divides into 3 rooms)
Trianon Ballroom—capacity 600
Mercury Ballroom—capacity 500
Gramercy Ballroom—capacity 490
Murray Hill Ballroom—capacity 420
Petite Trianon Ballroom—capacity 200

PARK LANE HOTEL / 36 Central Park South between Fifth and Sixth Avenues / 371-4000

Ballroom—capacity 175-200 (can be subdivided for smaller parties)

PIERRE HOTEL / Fifth Avenue at 61st Street / 838-8000

Grand Ballroom—capacity 700-850
Cotillion Room—capacity 300-360

PLAZA HOTEL / Fifth Avenue at 59th Street / 759-3000

Ballroom—capacity 650
Terrace Room—capacity 250
Baroque Room—capacity 200-300

REGENCY HOTEL / Park Avenue at 61st Street / 759-4100

Ballroom—capacity 150 (for cocktail reception, can hold up to 300)

ST. MORITZ HOTEL / 50 Central Park South between Fifth and Sixth Avenues / 755-5800

Quadrille Ballroom—capacity 200-300
Sky Garden Roof—capacity 100-125

ST. REGIS HOTEL / 2 East 55th Street between Fifth and Madison Avenues / 753-4500

St. Regis Roof—capacity 280-400
The Library—capacity 50-60 for cocktails, 25 for dinner.

WALDORF-ASTORIA HOTEL / Park Avenue between 49th and
50th Streets / 355-3000

Grand Ballroom—capacity 500–1500
Starlight Roof—capacity 300–600
Empire Ballroom—capacity 500
Hilton Ballroom—capacity 450
Astor Ballroom—capacity 350
Jade Room—capacity 350

Private Party Rooms

L' AIGLON / 13 East 55th Street between Fifth and Madison Avenues
753-7295

L'Aiglon, famous for its fine French cuisine, has a private party room,
which seats about 30 people. It can be reserved for luncheon and dinner.

BRUSSELS / 115 East 54th Street between Lexington and Park
Avenues / 758-0457

This fine restaurant is housed in an old mansion. The elegant public
dining that takes place on the ground floor is duplicated in its small
private rooms. There are two rooms, each holding up to 55–60 people.

CHRIST CELLA / 160 East 44th Street between Lexington and
Third Avenues / 697-2479

Good for entertaining a small business group. Steaks, chops and lobsters
are the specialties. Each of their three rooms holds 8–20 people.

FOUR SEASONS / 99 East 52nd Street between Lexington and Park
Avenues / 754-9494

The Four Seasons' private rooms are particularly good for cocktail parties
and private film and TV screenings. There are facilities for dinner parties
up to 50. Not as visually elegant as the main dining room, but with the
same fine food.

GIOVANNI RESTAURANT / 66 East 55th Street between
Madison and Park Avenues / Monday through Friday noon to 9:30
753–1230

This renovated town house is a good place to give private parties.
Giovanni Restaurant is quiet at night and bustling at lunch, but at all
times serves excellent Italian Continental cuisine. The private party
rooms hold up to 50 people and are perfect for luncheon, dinner or a
cocktail party, with or without music. Mr. Giovanni is one of the great
old restaurateurs and is generous with his personal attention.

LAURENT / 111 East 56th Street between Lexington and Park
Avenues / 753–2729

Laurent prepares some of the best food in town, accommodating private
dinners upstairs and down, with capacity up to 100.

L'ORANGERIE AT LE CIRQUE / 58 East 65th Street between
Madison and Park Avenues / 794–9292

L'Orangerie, a small architectural gem, is a perfect setting in which to
give an intimate party or dinner dance. The food is provided by Le
Cirque's kitchen. Their seating capacity is up to 150.

MAMMA LEONE'S RISTORANTE / 239 West 48th Street
between Broadway and Eighth Avenue / 586–5151

The Wine Cellars at Mamma Leone's are small rooms that work well for
informal gatherings with an Italian accent—the ambience and Italian
food (in abundance) are excellent. The three different Wine Cellars have
a capacity of from 50 to 200 guests.

*THE RAINBOW ROOM AND GRILL / 30 Rockefeller Plaza
at 49th Street between Fifth and Sixth Avenues / Dinner, daily,
5:00 to 11:30, Lunch, Sunday, noon to 2:30; orchestra plays from
4:00 P.M. to 1:00 A.M., Tuesday through Sunday / 757-9090*

The crown jewel of Rockefeller Center is the Rainbow Room and Grill.
The original Art Deco interiors and the 360° panorama of midtown
Manhattan make this 65th-floor restaurant one of the prettiest nightspots
in New York. Both rooms are private clubs in the daytime, but at night
are open to the public or are available for private parties. They are
suitable for cocktails and/or dinner, and/or dancing and/or
entertainment. Seating capacity ranges from 400 in the Rainbow Room
to 250 to 300 in the Rainbow Grill. For smaller parties of from 10 to
200 people, ask to see the private suites on the 64th floor.

*TAVERN ON THE GREEN / 40 West 67th Street at Central
Park West / 873-3200*

Warner LeRoy's latest masterpiece (he's also responsible for Maxwell's
Plum), set right in Central Park, has several beautiful rooms which can
be reserved for private parties. The view of the Park is enchanting, the
food is spectacularly presented and the decor has to be seen to be
believed.

*"21" CLUB / 21 West 52nd Street between Fifth and Sixth Avenues
582-7200*

On the second, third and fourth floors of this justifiably famous
institution are a series of small dining rooms in which many a top-drawer
N.Y. luncheon or dinner has taken place. Each of the rooms (whether its
capacity is 20 or 100 or more) has its own charming décor, but still
reflects the overall unique flavor of "21."

*WINDOWS ON THE WORLD / One World Trade Center
between West and Church Streets on Vesey Street / 107th floor
938-1111*

Even if the food at Windows on the World weren't excellent (which it
is), it would be worth having a party just to give your guests the
spectacular view of N.Y. which you can only get from the 107th floor of
the World Trade Center. Its Wine Cellar is a perfect room for
entertaining 20–30 people. To accommodate more, there are also
adjoining rooms which can be used separately or together, for lunches,
cocktail parties and dinners.

Passport Information

The U.S. Immigration and Naturalization Service maintains its N.Y. office in midtown. In the same Rockefeller Center building (630 Fifth Avenue) there is a passport photograph studio.

UNITED STATES PASSPORT OFFICE / 630 Fifth Avenue at 50th Street / Monday through Friday 8:00 to 4:30, Saturday 9:00 to 1:00 / 541–7710; recording with passport information: 541–7700

Photographic Equipment

Whether you are interested in renting 16-millimeter professionally-made film or equipping a complete darkroom, buying a simple or highly complex camera or just getting film developed, you'll find places below to meet your needs.

ALKIT CAMERA SHOPS, INC. / 866 Third Avenue between 52nd and 53rd Streets / Monday through Friday 8:00 to 6:00, Saturday 9:00 to 4:00 / 832–2101

Alkit has everything a shutterbug needs; in addition, they do repairs and develop film. You can also rent films here, along with a projector and other viewing supplies.

RENSAY, INC. / 49 East 58th Street between Madison and Park Avenues / Monday through Friday 8:45 to 5:45 / 688–0195

Rensay, Inc., is a neighborhood camera store that carries a wide range of cameras at every price level. In addition to selling film and developing it, they are marvelous about giving refresher courses on how to use cameras you already own.

*WAGNER PHOTOPRINT CO., INC. / 121 West 50th Street at
Sixth Avenue / Monday through Sunday 9:00 A.M. to 10:00 P.M.
245-4796*

This complete copy center is the place to go if you want great blow-ups
of photographs to use for a party. A tiny picture of a baby lying on a
bear rug, a graduation photo, a wedding portrait or any other sentimental
keepsake can be enlarged to almost any size that you're willing to pay for.

*WILLOUGHBY-PEERLESS CAMERA / 110 West 32nd Street
between Sixth and Seventh Avenues / Monday, Tuesday,
Wednesday 9:00 to 6:00, Thursday and Friday 9:00 to 7:00,
Saturday 9:00 to 6:00, Sunday 10:30 to 4:30 / 790-1800*

Willoughby's is one of the places where the professional photographers
hang out and often trade in their old cameras for new ones. So if you're
really into photography, this is where you can pick up used or new
equipment, starting with the cameras and going on up to the darkroom
supplies.

Picture Frames

New York framers work with artists and museum curators on
a day-to-day basis to make the frame an integral part of the
picture—no matter what the work's period or school. Also,
with photographs taking their place as true art today, more
and more attention is being paid to their framing. Obviously,
plastic, wood, velvet and leather frames are still available for
the family photos.

*A.P.F., INC. / 35 East 76th Street between Madison and Park
Avenues / Monday through Friday 9:45 to 5:30, Saturday 9:45—
closes early / 988-1090*

This master framer makes pretty frames at pretty prices for anything you
want framed. What they make is different from anyone else's because
they have their own factory.

*EMPIRE ARTISTS MATERIALS / 851 Lexington Avenue
    between 64th and 65th Streets / Monday through Friday 8:30 to
    6:00, Saturday 9:00 to 5:00 / 737–5002*

Harold at Empire brings his own artistic experience to any framing
project you bring to him. If you want something simply framed for an
office wall, he'll do it quickly and attractively; if you're looking for
something new, he'll work out an interesting original approach for the
object.

*HENRY HEYDENRYK, JR., INC. / 417 East 76th Street
    between First and York Avenues / Monday through Friday 9:30 to
    5:15, Saturday 9:30 to 3:30 / 249–4903*

Heydenryk is one of the most distinguished framers in the world, with
branches in the major cities of Europe. Being asked to frame a Renoir or
a Picasso doesn't faze this company at all—they do it all the time. Many
a minor piece of art has been made to look like a major one after being
framed by Heydenryk.

*KULICKE / 43 East 78th Street between Madison and Park Avenues
    Monday through Friday 10:00 to 5:00, Saturday 10:00 to 4:45
    254–0140*

Kulicke is the originator of the box-shaped Lucite frame where the
picture is all, i.e., no frame is visible. Graphic artists and printmakers
from across the country send their special pieces to Kulicke to be
framed. Though their forte is the contemporary frame, Kulicke also does
a good job in the more traditional mode.

*LEXINGTON ART GALLERY / 968 Lexington Avenue between
    70th and 71st Streets / Monday through Friday 9:00 to 6:00,
    Saturday 9:00 to 5:00 / 744–0229*

The Lexington Art Gallery does custom picture framing and also cleans
paintings.

*OLD ARTS / 805 Madison Avenue between 67th and 68th Streets
    Monday through Friday 9:30 to 5:30 / 744–7371*

Old Arts is known for beautiful velvet and silk made-to-order photograph
frames and matching silk pillows, desk accessories and wastebaskets.
Many of their materials are antique.

J. POCKER & SON / 824 Lexington Avenue at 63rd Street
Monday through Saturday 9:00 to 5:30 / 838-5488

At Pocker you can custom order, from numerous samples, a frame for any size oil painting, contemporary print or photograph. You may also choose from a large supply of ready-made frames in stock sizes. No job is too small or large for Pocker. On the second floor there is a collection of graphics which you can buy and then have framed, preferably, of course, by Pocker.

Printers

ABAT PRINTED NOVELTIES, INC. / 20 West 27th Street
between Broadway and Sixth Avenue / Monday through Friday
9:00 to 5:00 / 686-5540

Abat does speedy imprinting on paper products such as napkins and matches. They'll print on your product or theirs; theirs are limited, so if you want something special, bring your own.

NEMEC / 301 East 76th Street between First and Second Avenues
Monday through Friday 8:00 to 6:00, Saturday 8:00 to noon
744-6243

Nemec is a private press which prints stationery, charity folders, postcards, invitations, etc. They have some paper and envelopes in stock, but for highly stylized jobs it is better to search out and bring your own paper. Mr. Nemec's fast, reliable and not too expensive. He will show you a proof before he prints.

Records and Tapes

ALEXANDER'S / 731 Lexington Avenue between 58th and 59th Streets / Monday through Saturday 10:00 to 9:00, Sunday noon to 5:30 / 593–0880

If you know what you want, get your pop records and tapes here at good discounts. But be *sure* you know what you want because you can't play them until you get home, and there are no returns.

COLONY RECORDS / 1619 Broadway at 49th Street / Monday through Sunday 9:30 A.M. to 2:30 A.M. / 265–2050

This fabulous store is open seven days a week and has everything from records to tapes to sheet music. And if they don't have what you want, they'll get it.

SAM GOODY / 666 Third Avenue at 43rd Street / Monday through Friday 9:30 to 7:00, Saturday 9:30 to 6:30 / 986–8480
1290 Sixth Avenue at 51st Street / Monday through Friday 10 to 6:45, Saturday 9:30 to 6:00, Sunday noon to 5:00 / 246–8730

All the Sam Goody branches carry a goodly selection of records, tapes, radios, cassette machines and hi-fi equipment at reasonable prices.

KING KAROL RECORDS / 126 West 42nd Street between Sixth Avenue and Broadway / Monday through Saturday 9:00 A.M. to 9:00 P.M., Sunday 11:00 to 8:00 / 354–6880
940 Third Avenue between 56th and 57th Streets / Monday through Saturday 10:00 to 7:00 / 752–8650

King Karol carries all the new records, the golden oldies and a full stock of tapes.

LIBERTY MUSIC SHOP / 450 Madison Avenue at 50th Street
Monday through Saturday 9:00 to 6:00 / 753–0180

Liberty is one of the few places left where records and tapes may be listened to in private booths before buying. Not only do they stock all the current sounds, they also have vintage Sinatra, jazz and classical recordings. The store also sells quality television sets, radios and sound equipment.

Rentals

Virtually everything that can be bought in New York can also be rented. So why buy a bale of hay for a hayride when your five-year-old will only celebrate his or her fifth birthday once? Or the full regalia when your husband will play Napoleon at a costume ball? Or fifty cups and saucers when it's positively the last time you'll give a fund-raiser for anywhere near that number? Or a dozen potted palms to convince your co-workers that you have a green thumb the one time they'll visit your home? Or a gasoline-eating, seven-passenger limousine when you only want transportation for a bride and groom or an important customer for a single occasion?

ART

THE ART LENDING AND ADVISORY SERVICE OF
THE MUSEUM OF MODERN ART / 21 West 53rd Street
between Fifth and Sixth Avenues / Monday through Saturday
11:30 to 5:00, closed Wednesdays, Sunday 2:00 to 5:00, closed
weekends mid-June through Labor Day / 956–6114

Here, gathered from galleries throughout N.Y., are artworks by well-known and new painters, sculptors, photographers, lithographers, etc. For rentals (but not for purchases), a membership to the Museum is required. The rate for a two-month period is 10% of the purchase price, which then can be applied should you wish to buy.

BICYCLES

GENE'S / 300 East 77th Street at Second Avenue / Monday through
Friday 10:00 to 6:00, Saturday and Sunday 9:00 to 6:00
249–9239

If you are a kid, or feel like one, this is a good place to get good
two-wheelers for a spin around the Park.

CARS

AVIS / executive offices: 900 Old Country Road, Garden City, Long
Island / 516–222–3000; toll-free number to rent a car:
800–331–1212
Rental Locations:
310 East 64th Street between First and Second Avenues
240 East 54th Street between Second and Third Avenues
217 East 43rd Street between Second and Third Avenues

They say, "We try harder."

HERTZ RENT A CAR / executive offices: 660 Madison Avenue
752–2000; toll-free number to rent a car: 800–654–3131
Rental Locations:
327 East 64th Street between First and Second Avenues
310 East 48th Street between First and Second Avenues

Their slogan is, "We're Number One!"

COSTUMES

> BROOKS VAN HORNE / 117 West 17th Street at Sixth Avenue
> Monday through Friday 10:00 to 4:30, closed 12:00 to 1:00 for
> lunch / 989–8000

Since 1852 this shop has been the costumer for stage, screen and radio
performers, as well as for private dresser-uppers all over America. In
addition to stock items that include wigs and animal costumes, they will
make costumes to order.

FURNITURE

For furniture rentals, see page 89.

LIMOUSINES

> CAREY CADILLAC / 41 East 42nd Street between Madison and
> Vanderbilt Avenues / Suite 1710 / never closes / 937–3100

Carey is probably the best-known limousine rental company in New
York. It is an established and reliable company that supplies Cadillacs
with chauffeurs by the hour. The rate is $16 per hour (minimum of 3
hours), starting from the time the car leaves the garage until it returns,
with a 20% tip for the driver expected. (Tolls are extra, of course.)

> CHAUFFEURS UNLIMITED / 310 West End Avenue between
> 74th and 75th Streets / from 8:30 A.M. to 8:30 P.M.: 362–5354;
> after 8:30 P.M.: 874–3858

Hire a bonded driver to chauffeur your own car when your schedule
takes you uptown, downtown and crosstown. It's pleasant and surprisingly
reasonable for the service and comfort. This company will also supply its
own limousines for its chauffeurs to drive.

> REGENCY CHAUFFEURS SERVICE / 1980 East Tremont
> Avenue, Bronx / daily 9:00 A.M. to 10:00 P.M. / 792–9522

Regency is a reliable service that provides chauffeurs to drive your own
car.

SMITH LIMOUSINE / 137 West 56th Street between Sixth and Seventh Avenues / never closes / 247–0711

Because Smith Limousine service specializes in wedding parties, they have some white limousines that make it easy to identify your car in the usual sea of black limos. The rates are reasonable and the chauffeurs are dependable.

PARTY EQUIPMENT

Hayrides

As we keep saying, everything is available in New York—even hayrides.

CHATEAU STABLES, INC. / 608 West 48th Street between Eleventh and Twelfth Avenues / Monday through Sunday 8:00 to 6:00 / 246–0520

Pick up your guests in a hay wagon for a memorable hayride around Manhattan and deliver them to a favorite little restaurant or an ice-skating rink. The hay wagons accommodate up to twenty people, of all ages, at a flat rate of $150 Chateau Stables is open from April to December. Reservations are required.

For catering equipment see page 139.

SKI EQUIPMENT

SCANDINAVIAN SKI SHOP / 40 West 57th Street between Fifth and Sixth Avenues / Monday through Friday 9:30 to 7:30, Saturday 9:30 to 5:30 / 757–8524

If you want to spend all your time on the slopes instead of scrounging for equipment at the snow site, you can take your ski rental equipment with you. Scandinavian Ski Shop says, "Any skis we sell, we rent." And the same is true of their boots and poles. A $10 deposit is required; the rental price is determined by the caliber of the equipment you choose and the length of time of the rental.

TUXEDOS

BALDWIN FORMALS / 40 West 56th Street between Fifth and Sixth Avenues / Monday through Friday 8:45 to 6:00, Saturday 10:00 to 2:00 / 245–8190; 246–1782

If a man suddenly needs a white tie and tails, a tuxedo or morning suit, Baldwin's can instantly "suit" him. Once he has been outfitted, Baldwin will deliver his rented finery and pick it up the next day.

A. T. HARRIS CORP. / 419 Lexington Avenue between 43rd and 44th Streets / Monday through Friday 8:30 to 6:00, Thursday 8:30 to 7:00, Saturday 8:30 to 3:00 / 682–6325

Since 1892, Harris has come to the rescue of many a gentleman who forgot, or couldn't afford to buy, top hat and tails, tuxedos and morning coats. One-hour free parking is available.

Restaurants

You can eat your way around the world without ever leaving Manhattan. Whether your palate is exotic, ethnic or elephantine, it can be catered to by the most delicious, most expensive food purveyors on earth.

Though we all love and appreciate good food, we do not pretend that our taste buds are so finely attuned that we can discern a drop too much lemon in a sauce Hollandaise. Therefore, we happily leave the critiquing of restaurants and chefs to the experts, be their ratings in books or columns in the *New York Times*, the *Daily News*, the *New York Post*, *New York* magazine, *The New Yorker* or the *Village Voice*. So worry not Craig Claiborne, Mimi Sheraton, John Canaday, Seymour Britchky, Gael Greene and other estimable cuisine critics.

What we have done is to list here the restaurants that we frequent most. The choice of Where to eat in New York is quite often determined by Who you are meeting, What you are going to do before or after, When and Why the meal is taking place and How much you want to spend. (New York law requires restaurants to post their prices. If a menu isn't affixed to a restaurant window, just step inside and ask to see it.) In no way do we mean to imply that we use the fine restaurants listed below only at the times we are suggesting. We hope our list will inspire you to develop your own Who, What, Where and When strategy. It's always advisable to call for reservations in advance. If you are looking for places to take the youngsters, see Eats, page 49.

ART CROWD AND BOUTIQUE BUFFS

When hunger strikes in the midst of doing the art galleries and boutiques on Madison Avenue, there are some handy oases for slaking your thirst and sating your appetite.

*LA GOULOU / 28 East 70th Street between Madison and Park
Avenues / Monday through Saturday, Lunch, noon to 3:00, Dinner
6:00 to 11:30 / 988–8169*

La Goulou's pleasant atmosphere, combining the Parisian with the
Victorian, makes it a pretty place for lunch and dinner. The "art crowd"
generally orders from the food cart, but you can get hot dishes made to
order, and wine if you are in the mood for it.

*MADAME ROMAINE DE LYON / 32 East 61st Street between
Madison and Park Avenues / Monday through Saturday 11:30 to
3:00 / 758–2422*

When you've made your choice from *ten* closely-written pages listing
different omelettes, Madame will whip up a delicious one for you. Open
for lunch only. A woman alone will feel perfectly comfortable here and
get eating over with in a hurry, which will delight Madame.

*MAYHEW'S COUNTRY KITCHENS / 785 Madison Avenue at
66th Street / Monday through Friday 7:00 A.M. to 8:00 P.M.,
Saturday 8:00 to 5:00, Sunday 10:00 to 5:00 / 288–3781*

Mayhew's is basically a lunch counter with a few tables as well. It's an
agreeable stop for a quick good hamburger.

*POLO BAR / Westbury Hotel / Madison Avenue at 69th Street
Monday through Saturday, noon to 1:00 A.M.; Sunday, noon to
midnight / 535–2000*

The Polo Bar is perfect for a quick lunch in a quiet atmosphere, alone or
with a friend. There is a bar, but generally the salad and sandwiches are
dispensed at small tables and banquettes.

*PRONTO RISTORANTE / 30 East 60th Street between Madison
and Park Avenues / Monday through Saturday 11:30 to 11:30
421–8151*

The pasta at Pronto is made on the premises in full view. There are lots
of choices of Italian dishes and salads in this cheerful, bustling trattoria,
but the specialty is Pasta Pronto. It's always at a full boil and delivered
to the table *al dente*, or any way you choose. The back room (you'll
need a reservation) is slightly more formal with slightly less hustle.

*THE RIGHT BANK / 822 Madison Avenue at 69th Street
downstairs: Monday through Saturday 11:30 A.M. to 1:00 A.M.,
Sunday 1:00 P.M. to 1:30 A.M., upstairs: Monday through Saturday
5:30 to 10:45 / 650–1989*

The Right Bank is nice for lunch while doing the boutique belt. It has generously filled sandwiches and an excellent salad niçoise. You can sit at the bar, have a drink and a salad and make a quick getaway. The college group is apt to frequent the Right Bank at night to eat moderately priced but tasty dinners.

BEFORE AND AFTER THEATER AND FLICKS

If you are going to a show on Broadway, a concert at Carnegie Hall, the ballet at Lincoln Center or a movie on Third Avenue's Cinema Row, you'll find a good restaurant within walking distance.

*ALGONQUIN HOTEL / 59 West 44th Street between Fifth and
Sixth Avenues / Monday through Saturday, noon to 9:30; Supper
Buffet 9:30 to 12:30; Sunday Brunch, noon to 2:15; closed Sunday
for dinner / 687–4400*

You can talk here in a club-like atmosphere before and after theater. The late crowd eats and drinks mostly in the lobby and it's fun.

*DALY'S DANDELION / 1029 Third Avenue at 61st Street
Monday through Sunday 11:00 A.M. to 2:30 A.M. / 838–0780*

Cold draft beer, really good hamburgers and other good food can be had at Daly's Dandelion, no matter what time you come in. It is one of te best of many meeting and eating places that are consentrated on the East Side.

*FRANKIE AND JOHNNIE / 269 West 45th Street at Eighth
Avenue / second floor / Monday through Saturday 4:30 to 1:00 A.M.
245–9717*

A good steak place for which theater people have happily climbed a flight of stairs for decades. The scene is crowded, but the service is fast.

GINGERMAN / 51 West 64th Street between Central Park West and Broadway / daily, Lunch, noon to 4:00, Dinner 5:00 to 11:00 399–2358

The front room at the Ginger Man is generally filled with people on the way to or from Lincoln Center. It's a handy restaurant for theatergoers who are looking for a snack. This restaurant also serves full meals, but the service is slow for those on the go.

RUSSIAN TEA ROOM / 150 West 57th Street between Sixth and Seventh Avenues / Sunday through Friday 11:30 to 1:00 A.M., Saturday 11:30 A.M. to 2:00 A.M., Sunday Brunch, noon to 3:00 P.M. 265–0947

Almost directly adjacent to Carnegie Hall, this meeting place for actors and musicians is a good bet for lunch, tea or dinner, *après* concert or before. The hearty Russian food, such as borscht, beef Stroganoff and blinis, isn't just for peasants. Reservations recommended.

SARDI'S / 234 West 44th Street between Broadway and Eighth Avenue Monday through Saturday 11:30 A.M. to midnight / 221–8440

Sardi's is where Broadway performers are caricatured on the walls and congregated at the tables, sometimes to await the review of their new plays. Great fun after the theater on opening nights. Even on other nights it's a theatergoer's delight because its featured dishes, roast beef, chicken pot pie and lasagne, are instantly available.

BISTROS

A bistro is for when you don't want to dress up and do want a warm cozy atmosphere and lots of good food. Most of these places serve till late hours.

DICK EDWARDS / 132 East 61st Street between Lexington and Park Avenues / Monday through Sunday, noon to 4:00 A.M. 355–9010

When every other place has closed up for the night, Dick Edwards will still broil you a steak, chops or chicken. It's a dimly lit place, with a juke box playing saloon tunes as background music to the lively chatter around the bar.

ELAINE'S / 1703 Second Avenue at 88th Street / Monday through
Sunday, Lunch, noon to 4:00; Monday through Sunday, Dinner
6:00 to 2:00 A.M. / 831–9558

If you like to ogle writers and stage personalities, you'll see them as you
walk through the front room at Elaine's. Seafood, Italian-style, is her
specialty and it's quite good. Warning: it's not easy to get a table since
Elaine does not take reservations.

GINO'S / 780 Lexington Avenue between 60th and 61st Streets / daily,
noon to 10:30 / 838–9827

There is usually a brief wait for a table at this crowded restaurant, but
the excellent Italian food makes up for it. Black and white zebras
scamper over the red wallpaper, and the persons at the next table are
probably either Broadway or TV personalities. Great for Sunday lunch
and fairly priced. Reservations not accepted.

LE VEAU D'OR / 129 East 60th Street between Lexington and Park
Avenues / Monday through Saturday, noon to 10:00 / closed last
three weeks in August / 838–8133

Le Veau d'Or is a country French restaurant with everything on the
menu—from moules moutarde, to saumon poché and ris de veau—
perfectly prepared. Less expensive but more cramped than other of
N.Y.'s fine French restaurants. Even with the required reservation,
there's usually a wait.

PIETRO'S / 201 East 45th Street between Second and Third Avenues
Monday through Friday, noon to 10:30 / closed Saturday and
Sunday June through September, closed Sunday October through
May / 682–9760

It's worth the climb up the steep, narrow flight of stairs to savor this
luscious food. Virtually any veal, chicken or beef dish is done to order in
Italian style. It's small, crowded and noisy, but the food is super.
Expensive.

COCKTAILS AND...

These are convenient midtown meeting places which are delighted to serve you just cocktails or drinks after theater and/or food from breakfast through late-night supper. Many restaurants, such as "21," do a lively cocktail business, too.

KING COLE BAR / St. Regis Hotel / 2 East 55th Street, between Fifth and Madison Avenues / Monday through Friday, Breakfast 7:00 to 11:00; Lunch, noon to 2:30; Dinner 6:00 to 9:30; Saturday and Sunday 7:00 A.M. to 1:30 A.M. / 753-4500

Many a merry old soul has wet his whistle at the King Cole Bar, which is a pleasant wide-open room with comfortable banquettes, crisp white linen tablecloths, and a really super old-world atmosphere. It's as agreeable at breakfast as it is at luncheon, tea, cocktails, dinner and late in the evening for a snack or nightcap. Reservations are suggested for luncheon and dinner.

THE OAK ROOM BAR / Plaza Hotel / Fifth Avenue at 59th Street Monday through Sunday, Lunch, noon to 3:00; Dinner 6:00 to 10:00; Supper 10:00 to 11:30 / 759-3000

The Oak Bar is the place to meet for a quick drink. Its dark oak paneling and English decor exert a slightly calming influence on the hustle-bustle of the crowd.

THE PALM COURT / Plaza Hotel / Fifth Avenue at 59th Street Monday through Sunday, Breakfast 7:30 to 10:30; Coffee 10:30 to noon; Lunch, noon to 2:00; Drinks, Tea and Coffee 3:00 to 1:00 A.M. 759-3000

The Palm Court is an oasis in the lobby of the Plaza Hotel. It's a perfect meeting place for ladies at cocktail time. It also is one of the few spots in N.Y. that specializes in high tea.

TRADER VIC'S / Plaza Hotel / Fifth Avenue at 59th Street
Monday through Friday, Lunch 11:30 to 2:15; Monday through
Thursday, Dinner 5:00 to midnight; Friday and Saturday, Dinner
5:00 to 12:30; Sunday, Dinner 4:00 to 11:30 / 759–3000

If you are hungry at drink time, turn left into the bar at Trader Vic's. Here, amidst the Polynesian decor and background music, you can order butterfly shrimp, spareribs, beef on a skewer and other Orientalia. All these tidbits make a perfect accompaniment to an exotic rum-based drink replete with fresh fruit or even a gardenia. If you have no imagination, or a weak stomach, you can settle for a Chivas Regal on the rocks. Should you still be hungry and thirsty, you can adjourn to Trader Vic's dining room for lunch or dinner.

DON'T MISS

These are our special places for special occasions and special visitors. To miss them is to miss some of the unique flavor of our incredible City. You can go for lunch, cocktails, dinner or in the late evening, but go!

P. J. CLARKE / 915 Third Avenue at 55th Street / daily 11:30 A.M.
to 4:00 A.M. / 355–8857

P. J. Clarke's is the ultimate in hamburger joints. In this eating, drinking, meeting and making-merry place, it's very likely that the familiar face next to you is just who you think s/he is. Standing at the bar in the front room of P.J.'s, you can get a hamburger with your drink. Sitting at a table in the middle or back room, you can get a drink with your hamburger. In addition to great hamburgers, they have great chili, great draft beer (domestic and imported) and great atmosphere. Anytime that P.J.'s is open is *the* time to go there. It's always crowded. Reservations for the back room are recommended, but since it's not essentially an early dinner place, you might get in without one around 7 P.M.

LA CARAVELLE / 33 West 55th Street between Fifth and Sixth
Avenues / daily 12:15 to 10:30 / closed Saturday and Sunday
during summer / 586–4252

At Caravelle the food is perfect, which accounts for its rating as one of
the four great French restaurants in New York. The classic cuisine is
inspired by Henri Soulé's Pavillion, and the wine list can stand the
scrutiny of a *chevalier de taste-vin.* The surroundings are elegant; the
service is smooth and unobtrusive; the clientele is a roster of droppable
names. Caravelle is expensive and reservations are required.

LA CÔTE BASQUE / 5 East 55th Street between Fifth and
Madison Avenues / Monday through Saturday, noon to 10:30
688–6525

With the founding of Côte Basque, Henri Soulé set the style for a new
generation of fine French restaurants in New York. The Côte Basque
decor is beautiful, the lighting is flattering and the food, wine and
service are superior. Madame Henriette and her son Albert, who worked
so closely with the master, are still running La Côte Basque. As with all
our town's elegant eateries, the "Who's Who" sit in the front room.
Reservations are required.

LA GRENOUILLE / 3 East 52nd Street at Fifth Avenue / Monday
through Saturday, noon to 10:45 / closed six weeks during summer
752–1495

The fabulous bouquets of mixed fresh flowers that greet the eye as you
enter La Grenouille are works of art, and so is the food. Everything
selected from the menu will be perfectly presented, perfectly seasoned
and perfectly sauced. It's impossible to make a wrong choice of hors
d'oeuvres, or entrée. But whatever you have, save room for one of their
faultless soufflés.

LUTÈCE / 249 East 50th Street between Second and Third Avenues
Monday through Friday, Lunch, noon to 1:45; Monday through
Saturday, Dinner 6:00 to 10:00 / 752–2225

At Lutèce only the host's menu lists the prices. And it's just as well, for
this is probably the most expensive restaurant in New York. For the
guest blissfully ignorant of the tariff, Lutèce's charm and excellent
French food make it a fabulous dining experience. Reservations required.

PEARL'S / 38 West 48th Street between Fifth and Sixth Avenues
Sunday through Friday, Lunch, noon to 2:30; Dinner 5:00 to
10:30 / 586–1060

To us, Pearl's is the greatest Chinese restaurant in New York. You can
walk right by without noticing it, but you'll be sorry if you do. To miss
Pearl's is to miss her superb concoctions, such as *mu hsu* pork with *ping*
(translation: slivers of pork, ginger, bamboo and black mushrooms
blended together, ready for you to roll in thin rice crepes); *yook-soong*
(translation: another blending—this also of pork, ready for you to wrap in
chilled, crisp lettuce leaves). That's for openers. Her lemon chicken,
poached bass, crispy vegetables, Peking duck (order a day in advance)
and beef with lotus roots are just a few of her shareable main courses.
Pearl is open for lunch and for dinner, and it's *the* place to eat on
Sunday nights. Reserve well in advance if you have your heart set on a
particular day or time.

TAVERN ON THE GREEN / 40 West 67th Street at Central
Park West / daily, Lunch, noon to 2:30; Dinner 5:30 to 12:30
873–3200

This spectacular restaurant delights the eye of the beholder. Its jewel-like
setting in Central Park glitters with massive cut-crystal chandeliers and
highly polished brass; and its tables are covered with gaily flowered
cloths. The menu choices are enormous, considering the number of
people they serve daily in their many-splendored rooms.

"21" CLUB / 21 West 52nd Street between Fifth and Sixth Avenues
Monday through Saturday, noon to 12:30 A.M. / closed Saturday
May through Labor Day / 582–7200

For many New Yorkers, "21" is a home away from home. It is where
they celebrate, commemorate and congregate. The downstairs is noisy,
informal, gay and clubby. Normally the upstairs is quieter and more
formal. Lunch and dinner are served in both places. The food is tops, as
is the service. Reservations are required.

WINDOWS ON THE WORLD / One World Trade Center
between West and Church Streets on Vesey Street / 107th floor
Monday through Saturday, Lunch, noon to 2:15; Dinner 5:00 to
10:00; Sunday Buffet, noon to 7:30 / 938–1111

From Windows on the World, on a clear day you can see forever (after all, you're on the 107th floor). On a clear night, the twinkling lights of Manhattan, Brooklyn, Staten Island and New Jersey provide the view. By day and by night, you'll see the Statue of Liberty as she guards our harbor. There are many eating and drinking rooms here, and the food is good in all of them. Reservations well in advance are a must. If you're coming to New York from out-of-town, write just as soon as your plans are set.

HEALTH FOODS

These are the places for light lunches for rabbits.

GRASS / 1445 First Avenue at 75th Street / Sunday through Thursday
11:30 to 12:45, Friday and Saturday 11:30 to 1:45 A.M.
737–3328

It's the kind you eat, not the kind you smoke. Grass is good for natural foods, especially salads, but a more varied menu is also available. Moderate prices. Usually jammed.

HEALTHWORKS, INC. / 148 East 57th Street between Lexington
and Third Avenues / Monday through Friday 11:30 to 9:00,
Saturday 11:30 to 8:00 / 838–8370

The vegetarian, health-food addict, dieter and just plain salad-lover can all do their thing here at Healthworks—a modern. spanking clean, cafeteria-style restaurant. It offers a choice of several different salads each day with crispy fresh vegetables and fruits, seafood, etc., which you can enjoy with fresh fruit juices, a glass of wine and a slice of the best nut bread in town. Happily, all their healthful eats are inexpensive. It's hard to find a good "take-out" salad, but Healthworks has them and will even deliver.

LATE-NIGHT SPOTS

These places cater to night bloomers who are looking for food, disco-dancing, or just one more for the road.

BRASSERIE / 100 East 53rd Street between Lexington and Park Avenues / never closes; Saturday and Sunday, Brunch 11:00 to 5:00 / 751-4840

The Brasserie is open around the clock for sandwiches, omelettes and light snacks. More substantial courses are served at regular meal times. Reservations are accepted for dinner.

IRISH PAVILION / 130 East 57th Street between Lexington and Park Avenues / Wednesday through Saturday 11:30 A.M. to 3:00 A.M., Monday and Tuesday 11:30 A.M. to midnight / 759-9041

When Irish eyes are smiling, chances are it's because they are at the Irish Pavilion. This extraordinary place is a store, a bar and a restaurant. It stays open until the wee hours of the morning, with the customers singing right along with the paid entertainment. If you're not hungry, stop by anyway for a Harp Lager or an Irish coffee.

LA FOLIE / 21 East 61st Street between Fifth and Madison Avenues Monday through Saturday, Lunch 11:30 to 3:00, Dinner 6:00 to 12:00 / Disco from 10:30 or 11:00 to 3:00 A.M.; a $1.50 admission charge if you haven't had their dinner, which is served till 3:00 A.M. 765-1400

When you first see La Folie with its inlaid marble vestibule, its gigantic stained-glass mural behind the bar, the stainless-steel-looking walls surrounding the disco and its malachite-pillared dining room, you feel the place is indeed a folly. Happily, the French food served at lunch and dinner is classic, the wine list good, the music danceable at its late-night discotheque. You don't have to be rich to go here, but it's not a place for penny-counters.

RÉGINE'S / 502 Park Avenue between 59th and 60th Streets
Monday through Saturday 7:00 P.M. to 4:00 A.M. / 826–0990

Régine's, patterned after her place in Paris, is *the* N.Y. night place for the international set and the limousine trade. The art deco interior goes well with the beat, beat, beat of the music. You can dine beautifully but not cheaply on Régine's *haute cuisine*, in relatively peaceful surroundings till 10:30, when the disco opens. As the hour gets later the sound gets louder, the dancing more lively and even the lights vibrate off and on to the rhythm of the music. There is a $10 cover for the disco, unless you've dined at Régine's or hold one of her membership cards.

SHEPHEARD'S / 440 Park Avenue at 56th Street / Monday through
Saturday, Dinner 7:00 to 1:00, Monday through Friday, Lunch,
noon to 3:00 / 421–0900

Shepheard's, with its casbah atmosphere of glitter and cozy nooks, is a good late-night supper club; a cabaret that serves dinner until 1 A.M. After 9 P.M. there's a $3 cover charge for the show and dancing.

JIMMY WESTON'S RESTAURANT / 131 East 54th Street
between Lexington and Park Avenues / Monday through Friday,
Lunch, noon to 3:00; Monday through Sunday, Dinner 6:00 to
12:30 or 1:00 A.M. / two jazz groups play alternately every hour till
3:00 A.M. / 838–8384

Jimmy Weston's is as crowded at 12 midnight as Times Square is at 12 noon. The sound is constantly shifting from canned to live music as the scene shifts from dancing, eating or drinking to formal entertainment. Jimmy has a varied menu and lots of room for standees at his bar.

LUNCHEON

Over lunch in New York is when most of the business deals are made, when reporters get their scoops, when friendships flourish, when spirits are revived with good food and spirits, and when dozens of other things too important to mention also happen. In any case, the Lunch-Brunch places we have gathered here all have something in common: good food and the proprietors' willingness to let you linger over your coffee or help hurry you on your way (the choice is yours). How do we know? We learned it over lunch.

CAFÉ DES ARTISTES / 1 West 67th Street at Central Park West
Monday through Friday, Lunch, noon to 3:00; Monday through Saturday, Dinner 5:30 to 11:00; Sunday Brunch, noon to 3:00; Sunday Dinner 4:00 to 8:00 / 877–3500

Café des Artistes is a pretty restaurant with a relaxed and leisurely feeling. In fact, the atmosphere is somewhat better than the food. A wonderful spot for a lovely lazy Sunday brunch. The carts laden with food charmingly present a series of alternatives for each course.

CHÂTEAU RICHELIEU / 48 East 52nd Street between Madison and Park Avenues / Monday through Friday, Lunch, noon to 3:00; Monday through Saturday, Dinner 4:00 to 10:30 / 751–6565

This is a superb restaurant. On its comfortable banquettes you'll find a beehive of business men and women buzzing about big deals, yet the food manages to command its own share of attention. Everything you order comes just the way you hoped it would—and is beautifully served.

FOUR SEASONS / 99 East 52nd Street between Lexington and Park Avenues / Monday through Saturday, Lunch, noon to 3:00; Dinner 5:00 to 11:00; special Pre-Theater Dinner 5:00 to 6:30; After-Theater Dinner 10:00 to 11:00 / 754–9494

The name of this fashionable eating spot derives from the quarterly change of decor and menu that coincides with the change of seasons. (The Picassos and Mirós remain the same.) The choices offered on the menu are inventive and the service is excellent. There are two quite separate dining rooms: the 53rd Street side is centered around a large reflecting pool; the 52nd Street side is wood-paneled and has a large bar. The menu in the grill is simpler and less expensive, but for both rooms reservations are required. Only the fountain room is open for dinner.

L'AIGLON / 13 East 55th Street between Fifth and Madison Avenues
Monday through Saturday, Lunch, noon to 3:00; Monday through
Sunday, Dinner 5:30 to 11:00 / 753-7295

The place to sit in this nice restaurant is in the front room with the bar.
Don't despair if you are seated in the second room, however, for the fine
French food is the same. L'Aiglon's clientele is a cross section of
magazine biggies and Fifth Avenue shoppers. One of the great specialties
of the house is the fresh poached or grilled turbot.

LA PETITE CAFÉ / Sherry-Netherland Hotel / 781 Fifth Avenue at
59th Street / daily 7:00 A.M. to 1:00 A.M. / 355-2800

La Petite Café in the Sherry-Netherland Hotel is a very pleasant brunch
and lunch restaurant for watching Fifth Avenue strollers. The food here
isn't extraordinary but the chef salad is good and so are the eggs
benedict. It's the Fifth Avenue location that counts—for here you can
sit at a banquette, see the horse-drawn carriages around Central Park and
watch New Yorkers as they scurry by.

LE CIRQUE / Mayfair House / 58 East 65th Street between Madison
and Park Avenues / Monday through Saturday, Lunch, noon to
2:30; Dinner 6:00 to 10:30 / 794-9292

No monkey business about this "cirque," for it is probably the favorite
lunching place of many New York ladies. More charity benefits,
decorating schemes, wardrobe plans and just plain gossip have been
discussed over Le Cirque's white starchy napery than at any other Upper
East Side restaurant. The continental cuisine and service are first class.
The house and the chicken salads are the ladies' luncheon staples, but
there's more substantial fare for the men. Reservations are required.

LE MADRIGAL / 216 East 53rd Street between Second and Third
Avenues / Monday through Friday, noon to 11:00; Saturday 6:00
to 11:00 / 355-0322

Slightly off the regular track for the lunch bunch, Le Madrigal is popular
with publishers, editors and literary agents. The long narrow dining room
is filled with flowers, and the garden tables are one of New York's most
pleasant summer oases. The food, wine and service are all superior.
Reservations required.

*LE MISTRAL / 14 East 52nd Street between Fifth and Madison
Avenues / Monday through Saturday, Lunch, noon to 3:00,
Dinner 5:00 to 11:00 / 421–7588*

Le Mistral is another fine spot where all the amenities of a good French
restaurant can be found. The luncheon crowd is usually comprised of
Madison Avenue persons, using their expense accounts with style.

*MAXWELL'S PLUM / 1136 First Avenue at 64th Street / daily,
noon to midnight; café open till 1:30 A.M. / 628–2100*

The Tiffany-glass ceiling, the hanging plants, the cozy sidewalk seating
area and the Victorian background are about all that's old-fashioned
about this restaurant. Young people are packed three and four deep
around its bar, couples are gathered in its middle room, and up another
few steps are mother and fathers with *their* mothers and fathers and
their grandchildren. In other words, Maxwell's Plum is all things to all
people. The huge hamburgers are excellent, and so is the rest of the
food. One look at its proprietor, Warner LeRoy, is all you need to know
that he *cares* about food.

*NEW YORK EXCHANGE RESTAURANT / 541 Madison
Avenue between 54th and 55th Streets / Monday through Friday,
Lunch 11:30 to 2:30; Tea 3:30 to 5:00; Dinner 5:15 to 7:30
753–2330*

The N.Y. Exchange is one of the homiest restaurants in New York for
lunching alone. The quality of the food is wholesome, and everything is
homemade. Tea is a treat.

*ORSINI'S / 41 West 56th Street between Fifth and Sixth Avenues
Monday through Saturday, Lunch, noon to 3:00; Dinner 5:30 to
10:00 / 757–1698*

Style-setters, fashion magnates and their faithful observers flock upstairs
for a summit lunch in a garden atmosphere at Orsini's six days a week.
The Orsini brothers' own wine is served in carafes; the scampi is sautéed
over a flame at tableside; the arrugala salad is absolute perfection and
table-hopping is *de rigueur*. Dinner is also served downstairs at night, but
it's more fun upstairs for either meal. If you want to eat more quickly, or
can't get a reservation on 56th Street, try the new Orsini's at Bonwit
Teller, on the second floor, for lunch (or for dinner on those nights the
store is open).

MAIN EVENT

When just eating with our friends is the thing, we choose these restaurants for their fine food, carefully chosen wine lists, lovely surroundings with fresh flowers, soft lighting and comfortable seating, all of which makes it possible to linger over dinner and enjoy good conversation.

BOX TREE / 242 East 50th Street between Second and Third Avenues Monday through Saturday 12:30 to 11:00 / 758–8320

There are only eight tables in this charming little spot, so booking a table days in advance is mandatory. Though the choice of dishes is limited, everything is excellently prepared to order.

CHEZ PASCAL / 151 East 82nd Street between Lexington and Third Avenues / Monday through Saturday, Dinner only, two sittings 7:00 and 9:30 / 249–1334

Chez Pascal is especially popular with those who live uptown. It is one of New York's excellent but smaller French restaurants, so reservations must be made days in advance.

HERMITAGE RESTAURANT / 251 East 53rd Street at Second Avenue / Monday through Friday, Lunch, noon to 2:30; Monday through Saturday, Dinner 6:00 to 10:30 / 421–5360

The pleasant Tudor-style French restaurant is a descendant of the great Henri Soulé's school of cuisine and service. The first courses are attractively presented, and if you're not afraid of taking the edge off your appetite, try the hors d'oeuvres *varié*. The entrées are perfectly cooked to your order and sauced with a sure hand. *Les poissons* are *toujours* fresh and delectable, and the wine cellar is excellent.

KATJA / 225 East 58th Street between Second and Third Avenues Monday through Friday, noon to midnight; Saturday 6:00 to midnight / 751–5488

Katja is a pretty, pretty restaurant with good food, elegantly served. The staff is attentive to one and all and, if they have room, they will happily give you a table without a reservation.

LAURENT / 111 East 56th Street between Lexington and Park Avenues / Monday through Saturday, noon to 10:30; Sunday 5:00 to 10:30, except July and August / 753–2729

Laurent boasts an excellent menu of traditional French food. Hard to beat are their salmon mousse, roast rack of lamb and venison steak. The wine list is superb, the ambience pleasant, the service good and the clientele attractive. In the bar (a room with nicely spaced tables) you may eat as well as drink. Reservations are required, except in the bar.

LE CYGNE / 53 East 54th Street between Fifth and Madison Avenues Monday through Friday, Lunch, noon to 2:00; Dinner 6:00 to 10:00; Saturday, Dinner 6:00 to 10:00 / 759–5941

Le Cygne is one of the top French spots, with a *prix fixe* menu for both lunch and dinner. Its food is of the Pavillion school, its ambience is attractive and its service is excellent. Reservations required.

QUO VADIS / 26 East 63rd Street between Madison and Park Avenues / Monday through Saturday, noon to 11:00 / 838–0590

Quo Vadis has the grandeur and elegance of restaurants of old, with its red velour banquettes, crisp white napery, freshly set tables and a superb chef. Most of their menu dishes are cooked to your order when you arrive, be it for a leisurely lunch or dinner. If it's a roast chicken you want, so say when you reserve and it will be done. The "shoppers" like to eat at tables situated in the Quo Vadis Bar room, but sit where you will, the salads and fish and meats are just great, as are the wine list, the owners and the waiters.

OFF THE BEATEN TRACK

These restaurants are off our beaten track and for us to visit them is an expedition. Because all cab drivers do not know their way around Greenwich Village and Brooklyn, it is wise to ask for directions when you call to make reservations.

COACH HOUSE / 110 Waverly Place between Washington Square West and Sixth Avenue / Tuesday through Sunday, noon to 10:00 777–0303

The Coach House is considered by many critics to be the best restaurant in Greenwich Village. The decor is Colonial, the fare is hearty and the service is excellent.

GIORDANO / 409 West 39th Street between Ninth and Tenth
Avenues / Monday through Friday, noon to midnight; Saturday
5:30 to midnight; Sunday 2:30 to 10:30 / 947–9811

Really superb Italian food is served here. There is no menu: the maitre d'
recites a seemingly endless list of dishes until he hits upon something
that strikes your fancy, which is then cooked to perfection. The
ambience is pleasant with three different dining areas, and the location
(just at the entrance of the Lincoln Tunnel) makes it a perfect stopping
place for the New Jersey-bound (there's a place to park), a favorite lunch
place for Seventh Avenue designers and an ideal dining place for those
Manhattanites who want to go off the beaten track.

GROTTA AZZURRA / 387 Broome Street, corner of Mulberry
Street / Tuesday through Sunday, noon to midnight / 226–9283

At the Grotta Azzurra you'll find delectable Italian specialties reasonably
priced. Wine and beer are the only spirits available. They do not take
reservations, and there is usually a wait for a table.

PETER LUGER / 178 Broadway, corner of Driggs Avenue, Brooklyn
Sunday through Thursday 11:45 to 9:30, Friday 11:45 to 11:00,
Saturday 11:45 to 11:15 / 387-7400; 384-9100

Just over the Williamsburg Bridge in Brooklyn, Peter Luger's has been
serving superior food since 1887, and there is no better steak house in all
of New York. It unpretentiously concentrates on presenting perfect
steaks, chops, potatoes and salad. Reservations required.

OPEN ON SUNDAY

These are the hard-to-find restaurants that we rely on when our otherwise
dependables say, "We're Never Open on Sunday."

ALGONQUIN HOTEL / See page168.

BEEFBURGER / See page 185

BRASSERIE / See page 176.

CAFÉ DES ARTISTES / See page 178.

CHARLIE'S PIZZA / See page 185.

P. J. CLARKE / See page 172.

COACH HOUSE / See page 182.

ELAINE'S / See page 170.

GINGERMAN / See page 168.

GINO'S / See page 170.

GRASS / See page 175.

L'AIGLON / See page 179.

LAURENT / See page 182.

MAXWELL'S PLUM / See page 180.

J. G. MELON'S / See page 189.

NATHAN'S / See page 186.

PEARL'S / See page 174.

PLAZA HOTEL / Oak Room Bar / Palm Court / Trader Vic's / See page 171.

RUSSIAN TEA ROOM / See page 169.

ST. REGIS HOTEL / King Cole Bar / See page 171.

SEA FARE OF THE AEGEAN / See page 187.

TAVERN ON THE GREEN / See page 174.

WESTBURY HOTEL / Polo Bar / See page 167.

WINDOWS ON THE WORLD / See page 175.

QUICK FOOD

Some days the name of the game is "Hurry!" and these are the places where you can eat practically on-the-run. Nearly every department store has a place for a quick bite and we've noted two in particular that we use the most often.

BEEFBURGER / 804 Lexington Avenue at 62nd Street / Monday through Saturday 7:00 A.M. to 10:00 P.M. / 838–3580

The Beefburger is in Bloomingdale country—just two short blocks away from the famed store, but it also is a neighborhood haunt. It's a cook-to-order place, clean, attractive and with nice waiters. You can quickly get breakfast (eggs any style and sweet rolls or muffins), lunch, tea or dinner. As the name implies, the specialties of the house are hamburgers, and they *are* good. Beefburger has tables and counter service.

BIGI'S BITE / Bergdorf Goodman / 754 Fifth Avenue at 58th Street sixth floor / Monday through Saturday 10:00 to 6:00, Thursday 10:00 to 8:00 / 753–7300

Bigi's Bite is no bigger than a counter. Here you can get a tasty sandwich or salad, and be back to your shopping within minutes.

CHARLIE'S PIZZA / 140 Lexington Avenue at 58th Street Monday through Sunday 9:00 A.M. to 4:00 A.M. 421–5469

Charlie's makes the best fast pizza in town and sells it by the slice or the whole pie. You can eat it at their counter, munch it as you stroll, or have it delivered at any hour of the day or way into the night.

H. H. HICKS AND SON / 16 East 49th Street between Fifth and Madison Avenues / Monday through Friday 8:00 to 7:00, Thursday 8:00 A.M. to 9:00 P.M., Saturday 11:00 to 7:00 / 688–5552

Wonderful hot fudge sundaes, milk shakes and malteds—that's what Hicks is all about. They also serve sandwiches and salads, and the quick counter service makes it a convenient stop-over if you get hungry in Saks Fifth Avenue country.

*LA POTAGERIE / 554 Fifth Avenue between 45th and 46th Streets
Monday through Saturday 11:00 to 9:00 / 586–7790*

At La Potagerie three rich and flavorful soups are offered daily, together with cheese, fruit, wine and dessert if you choose. This soup cafeteria is good for a quick lunch near Saks Fifth Avenue, and a fine place if you want to lunch alone. It's best to get there early, though the line moves quickly.

*NATHAN'S / 6 East 58th Street between Fifth and Madison Avenues
daily 10:30 A.M. to midnight, weekends stays open a little later
751–9060
879 Third Avenue between 53rd and 54th Streets / Monday
through Thursday 6:30 A.M. to 2 A.M., Friday 6:30 A.M. to 4 A.M.,
Saturday 11 A.M. to 4 A.M., Sunday, noon to midnight / 752–6881*

You really have to see Nathan's to believe it. Of course they have the famous Nathan's hot dog, but they also serve fried shrimp, clams and potatoes, broiled hamburgers, fish, chili, tomatoes, salads and, and, and, and . . . On the main floor the service is cafeteria-style and they do a deservedly big business. Most people eat at stand-up counters but if you want to sit and be served, the downstairs is set up to accommodate you.

*OLD FASHIONED MR. JENNINGS / Bonwit Teller / 721 Fifth
Avenue at 56th Street / ninth floor / Monday through Saturday
10:00 to 6:00, Thursday 10:00 to 8:00 / 355–6800*

Here you sit at a counter—though there are a few tables—to have a sweet. The sundaes are great, and if you want to precede one with a sandwich, you'll find a limited tea-roomy selection. It's a good place for a lunch alone.

SEAFOOD

It's not the rivers around our tight little island of Manhattan that yield up our seafood, but it's from nearby waters that the best catches are hauled in to stock these three restaurants.

GLOUCESTER HOUSE / 37 East 50th Street between Madison and Park Avenues / Monday through Friday, Lunch, noon to 2:30; Dinner 5:30 to 9:30; Saturday and Sunday, noon to 9:45 755-7394

The businessmen in this area jam Gloucester House at noon but women often go there, too. The fish is freshly cooked and appetizingly presented. The calories you save by eating fish are quickly squandered on their delicious homemade biscuits. Their standards are high, and so are their prices.

OYSTER BAR / Plaza Hotel / Fifth Avenue at 59th Street / Monday through Saturday 11:30 to 1:00 A.M. / 759-3000

The Oyster Bar at the Plaza is a small attractive place for fish-lovers. The lighting is dim and conducive to quiet conversation and unrushed eating. Their menu isn't vast, but what they have is good.

SEA FARE OF THE AEGEAN / 25 West 56th Street between Fifth and Sixth Avenues / Monday through Saturday, noon to 11:00; Sunday 1:00 to 11:00 / 581-0540

Sea Fare of the Aegean is one of the best seafood restaurants in New York. If you want codfish, haddock, halibut, herring, mackerel, red snapper, sardines, shad, smelts, trout, tunafish, bass, bluefish, Dover sole, flounder, salmon, scallops, lobsters—in other words, anything catchable— you'll find it cooked to perfection at this pleasant lunch and dinner multileveled place. Sea Fare also has fish soups and all shellfish when they're in season. It's large enough to sometimes take customers without a reservation, but if you have your heart set on fish, it's better to reserve.

SMALLISH PLACES AT SMALLISH PRICES

Smallish dining places for diverse diners—college kids on a spree, the Graduate and his Mrs. Robinson or other non-expense-account diners who have sophisticated taste buds and are looking for unsophisticated prices. Let the blurb be your guide as to which restaurant would suit your taste.

CAFÉ EUROPA / 347 East 54th Street between First and Second
Avenues / Monday through Friday, Lunch, noon to 3:00; Monday
through Saturday, Dinner 5:00 to 11:00 / 755–0160

Brioche is the specialty of the house, with almost anything imaginable prepared within the flaky crust for a pleasant, unusual menu.

CHARLEY O'S / 33 West 48th Street between Fifth and Sixth
Avenues / Monday through Saturday 11:30 to 11:00 / 582–7141

Pigs' knuckles, corned beef, shrimp, boiled ham with cabbage, and draft beer are the specialties of this marvelous, though crowded, eatery. And sure if you order their well-laced coffee you'll be after knowin' you're in 'n Irish pub.

EL PARADOR / 325 East 34th Street between First and Second
Avenues / Monday through Saturday 5:00 to 11:00 / 679–6812

El Parador is the spot for spicy Mexican food. Reservations are not taken, so you may have to stand and wait.

IL VAGABONDO / 351 East 62nd Street between First and Second
Avenues / Monday through Friday, Lunch, noon to 3:00; Monday
through Sunday, Dinner 5:30 to midnight / 832–9221

Where, outside of Italy, can you play a game of boccie between courses? At Il Vagabondo, that's where. This restaurant is housed in a remodeled brownstone. Its rooms vary in size, but the steaks and pasta and other goodies are excellent at every table—and it's hard to get one without a wait.

*LE MOAL / 942 Third Avenue between 56th and 57th Streets
Monday through Saturday, Lunch, noon to 3:00; Dinner 5:30 to
11:00; Sunday Dinner 5:30 to 11:00 / 688–8860*

Le Moal is one of the best of the moderately priced French bistros.
Throughout the years its customers have appreciated the escargot
bourguignon, canard à l'orange and mousse au chocolat.

*J. G. MELON'S / Third Avenue at 74th Street / Monday through
Sunday, 11:30 A.M. to 4:00 A.M. / 744–0585*

At J. G. Melon's, the waiters are as young and polite as the customers.
The fare is charcoal-broiled hamburgers and steaks. The time to go is
whenever you're hungry. If you get hungry at the same time as others,
you may have to wait for a table.

*NICOLA'S / 146 East 84th Street between Lexington and Third
Avenues / Monday through Sunday 6:00 P.M. to midnight
249–9850*

One of Elaine's* aides de-camped, and opened his own spot. His food is
Italian, and the young literati who frequent his place think it's
sensational. It's a good idea to make a reservation.

*Elaine of Elaine's Restaurant

STEAK HOUSES

There are literally hundreds of good steak houses in New York. We are
"steering" you to those listed below for, besides having good steak, each in
its own way is unique.

*CHRIST CELLA / 160 East 46th Street between Lexington and
Third Avenues / Monday through Friday, Lunch 11:45 to 4:00;
Monday through Saturday, Dinner 5:00 to 10:30 / 697–2479*

Christ Cella is for hearty eaters. The steaks, chops and fish—mainstays
of their menu—arrive sizzling hot from the kitchen, accompanied by the
best hashed brown potatoes in town. This is a bustling restaurant where
the lighting and decor is of the no-nonsense school that seems to suit
men more than women. Christ Cella does a lively bar business, as
customers without a reservation nearly always have to sit and wait.

GALLAGHER'S STEAK HOUSE / 228 West 52nd Street
between Broadway and Eighth Avenue / Monday through Saturday
11:30 A.M. to midnight / 245–5336

Gallagher's is a spacious beehive of men at lunch time. Because of its proximity to West Side theaters and its good food, couples crowd this pleasant bar and grill at night. The steaks and chops are grilled to order and roast sirloin is a specialty of the house. The beef-in-the-raw that you see encased in a glass cooling room as you enter is being aged to perfection for Gallagher's beef-loving patrons.

PALM RESTAURANT / 837 Second Avenue between 44th and 45th
Streets / Monday through Saturday, noon to 11:45 / closed first
two weeks in July / 682–9515

The Palm Restaurant is a rambling, sort of tacky-looking place that is a favorite of everyone's—from the politicians to the literati. Its marvelous steaks, lobsters, scallops, home fries and friendly down-to-earth atmosphere compensate for the crowding, which makes eavesdropping a necessity rather than a choice.

PEN AND PENCIL / 205 East 45th Street between Second and
Third Avenues / Monday through Friday 11:45 to 11:30, Saturday
and Sunday 4:30 to 11:30 / 682–8660

Pen and Pencil is a favorite steak house of the people who write the news and the people who make it. Here the seating is comfortable; the steaks, roasts and chops are cooked the way you want them; the waiters are pleasant; the customers are convivial.

Secretarial Service

CLARK UNLIMITED PERSONNEL / 527 Madison Avenue at
54th Street / Monday through Friday 8:30 to 6:00 / 759–1905

A wide assortment of secretarial and clerical services from a large pool of well-tested, experienced people. Proofreaders and typists who edit are available, besides conventional office help. All work is done on your premises. Arrangements can be made for weekends.

LAURA DEE / 24 West 57th Street between Fifth and Sixth Avenues
581–7550

Miss Dee and Miss Resnick provide fast, personalized and reasonably priced secretarial services on their premises. Typing is accurate, and multiple copies can be run off. They also will stuff, address and mail envelopes in quantity.

WORLD-WIDE BUSINESS CENTRES / 575 Madison Avenue
between 56th and 57th Streets / 486–1333

Every service any office needs from typing to photocopying. The work is done on the premises, and their services are available daily, evening and on weekends. Dictation is taken, but an estimate of time needed must be stated and an appointment booked.

Shoes

The best way to enjoy New York is on foot, so shoe stores in Manhattan do a sprightly business. Every kind of shoe is available somewhere in our city—from nurses' shoes to orthopedic, Earth shoes, clogs and made-to-order, to name a few. All department stores have shoe departments, with Saks Fifth Avenue's the most comprehensive. The stores we list below specialize in the imported shoes one usually finds only in foreign capitals. Take a walk; if your feet get tired, go in, take a rest and try on a new pair of shoes.

HELENE ARPELS / 665 Madison Avenue between 60th and 61st
Streets / Monday through Friday 10:00 to 6:00, Saturday 10:00 to
5:00 / 755–1623

Expensive shoes that are hard to beat for style and elegance. It is difficult to find more beautiful shoes than those designed by Helen Arpels and made in Italy. Her classic bedroom slippers come in a multitude of colors in leather or velvet, which makes them useful in the bedroom or at the beach. She also carries a full range of *sportif*, day and evening footwear with prices starting at $125, and sizes from 4 1/2 AA to 10 1/2 B. Her satin evening slipper with its long-stemmed jeweled flower is the ultimate Cinderella shoe.

CHANDLER'S / 695 Fifth Avenue between 54th and 55th Streets Monday through Saturday 10:00 to 6:00, Thursday 10:00 to 7:30 688-2140

A large selection of reasonably priced shoes, usually copied from expensive models, from huaraches to high-platform clogs, stenciled high-heeled boots, basic bedroom slippers and plain white evening shoes for dyeing. Prices start at $16.99 for shoes and $39.99 for boots—and these are not sale prices.

DELMAN SHOE SALON / Bergdorf Goodman / 754 Fifth Avenue between 57th and 58th Streets / Monday through Saturday 10:00 to 6:00, Thursday 10:00 to 8:00 / 759-7600

Delman has a stable of shoe designers. The international entries include Tannio Crisci and Amalfi of Italy, Givenchy and Charles Jourdan of France, Edward Rayne of London, and American designers such as Geoffrey Beene, Anne Klein, David Evins and Halston. In the comfortable, old-world atmosphere of their salon you can be fitted with morning, noon or nighttime shoes, sandals or boots, sizes 6 to 10 narrow, 5 to 10 medium, at prices from $36 to $175. A plus is the repair and refurbishing service for your slightly tired and worn Delman shoes. And the man who dyes their evening shoes is one of the best.

FERRAGAMO / 717 Fifth Avenue at 56th Street / Monday through Saturday 9:30 to 6:00, Thursday 9:30 to 7:00 / 751-2520

The Ferragamo family of Florence has put its distinctive stamp on all aspects of this modern steel and glass shop on Fifth Avenue. The handsome leather shoes and handbags, all made in Florence, are of Ferragamo design and manufacture. Shoe (and boot) sizes run from 3B to 11B, prices from $50 to $160. If you are looking for classic good looks and understatement, this shop is for you. Even the beautifully made clothes (mostly of pure silk or wool) have the unique Ferragamo look.

CHARLES JOURDAN / 700 Fifth Avenue at 55th Street / Monday through Saturday 10:00 to 6:00, Thursday 10:00 to 8:00 / 541-8440

Charles Jourdan is famous for the most avant shoes and boots around, all imported from France and Italy. Whatever style Bazaar and Vogue are forecasting, be it the sky-high stiletto heel, the flat, flat sandal or the clunky clog, you can be sure Jourdan already stocks it. And although the classic Jourdan pump changes from season to season, it is always recognizable for its sleekness and beauty. Handbags, scarves and a small shoe selection for men are at CJ too. Prices run from $32 to $170, but if you're a shoe cognoscente, Jourdan shoes at any price are a joy. Sizes from 4 1/2 AA to 10 1/2 B.

LADY CONTINENTAL / 836 Madison Avenue at 69th Street
Monday through Saturday 10:00 to 6:00 / 988–0110

Lady Continental has the imported classic moccasin with the golden bit in both high- and low-heel versions. The Chanel shoe with its black-tipped toe is another stock item here. New things are always arriving at this style-conscious boutique. Their shoes are always light in weight and ladylike in looks. Sizes run from 6B to 9 1/2M. Prices run from $40 to $75 for shoes; for boots, from $160 to $190.

MARIO OF FLORENCE / 767 Fifth Avenue between 58th and
59th Streets / Monday through Saturday 10:00 to 5:30 / 832–7931

Mario, as is apparent from the store's name, imports all its footwear from Florence. The shoes are light as a feather, mostly made by hand, and in classic styles and colors. The shop has handbags to match many of its shoes. You have to almost empty your own bag to buy from Mario since the prices run from $88 to $400, but a lot of ladies feel they are worth every lira. Mario carries shoes in sizes from 4 1/2B to 11B.

I. MILLER SHOES / Fifth Avenue at 57th Street / Monday through
Saturday 9:30 to 6:00, Thursday 9:30 to 7:00 / 581–0062

The home of the famous David Evins shoes and the equally well-known I. Miller label. This branch of I. Miller carries a large selection and stock of shoes, so if you see something you like they are almost certain to have it in the size and color you want. The sizes of shoes range from 4B to 11B; prices for shoes range from $50 to $70, for boots from $60 to $200. After you've shoe-shopped, you can clothes-shop in their General Store just one flight up.

MILLER EYE / 11 East 54th Street between Fifth and Madison
Avenues / Monday through Saturday 9:30 to 6:00, Thursday 9:30
to 7:00 / 753–2577

This is I. Miller's store for the young trade. They have boutique items mixed with their platforms, sandals, rain boots and other fun footgear, but their absolute specialty is Jacques Cohen's Espadrille collection. His classic model is here in every color under the sun, and most of his other styles come in at least five or six shades. Sizes run from 5B to 10B—and prices from $18 to $96.

Silver

Most gift shops, both in and out of department stores, carry many sterling and plated silver pieces. Those we have written about are the stores or the departments that are specialists in silver and those whose silver wares are unique.

B. ALTMAN & COMPANY / Fifth Avenue between 34th and 35th Streets / Monday through Saturday 10:00 to 6:00, Thursday 10:00 to 8:00 / 689–7000

The flatware at Altman's is made by the leading American silver manufacturers, which include International, Gorham, Wallace, Lunt and Frank Smith. They range in price from $110 to $200 for a dinner setting of five pieces. They also carry sterling silver coffee and tea sets.

BUCCELLATI / 703 Fifth Avenue at 55th Street / Monday through Saturday 9:30 to 5:30 / 755–4975

Buccellati designs and hand-makes all of its own silver in Italy. The silver is heavily chased, baroque in feeling and always distinctively Buccellati. In addition to flatware (which starts at $108 per five-piece place setting and runs to $550), this fine Italian silversmith also excels in occasional pieces of silver, such as candelabra, gem-incrusted boxes, sculptures of flora and fauna, tea and coffee services and the like. They do vermeil, but reluctantly, explaining that it takes five or six coats of 18-carat gold to get it perfect, and then it doesn't stay on very long with normal usage.

CARTIER / Fifth Avenue at 52nd Street / second floor / Monday through Saturday 10:00 to 5:30 / 753–0111

Cartier carries twenty-six different American flatware patterns which are individual and difficult to find elsewhere. Prices for a five-piece place setting start at $205 and go up to $400. That silver which is made by Old Newbury Crafters is signed by the artist, and that made by Porter Blanchard is all handwrought and hand-finished. Cartier also imports the well-known French plated silver, Christofle. In addition to a good selection of sterling accessories with a contemporary look, the traditional Revere bowls can be found here.

CHRISTOFLE / Baccarat, Inc. / 55 East 57th Street between Madison and Park Avenues / Monday through Saturday 9:30 to 5:30 826–4100

The prices for Christofle's sterling silver place settings start where most others leave off ($400) and soar on up to $2,000—and there is a six-month wait besides. The specialty of the shop, however, is their heavy French silverplate, which runs from $50 to $85 per place setting. Coffee and tea sets are also available, in both plate and sterling. C'est merveilleux!

JEAN'S SILVERSMITHS, INC. / 16 West 45th Street between Fifth and Sixth Avenues / Monday through Friday 9:00 to 5:30 697–0367

Jean's has a large selection of discontinued silver patterns, to say nothing of lots of new ones at a vastly lower price than regular silver shops. It's perfect for replacing lost teaspoons and other pieces. It may take them a year, or sometimes even longer, to find a specific pattern, but eventually they do. You can depend on Jean. And if you're really lucky, it's right there in stock now.

GEORG JENSEN / Madison Avenue between 57th and 58th Streets / Monday through Saturday 10:00 to 6:00, Thursday 10:00 to 7:00 / 935–2800

Ten patterns of the sterling silver flatware at George Jensen's are made in Denmark and most of them are highly copied by others.

But Jensen's continues to carry its classic designs, and those who own the originals know the difference. Depending upon pattern and weight of silver, the price of a five-piece place setting starts at $250.

MAYER SILVERWARE / 136 East 57th Street between Lexington and Third Avenues / Monday through Friday 9:30 to 5:00, Saturday 10:00 to 5:00 / 759–4173

Mayer's has place settings by the American silversmiths in sterling silver and in silverplate. It also carries hundreds of little silver and silverplated items, such as salt and pepper shakers, pepper mills, ash trays, porringers, sugar and creamers, dinner bells, toast racks, sugar tongs, ice tongs, ice buckets and on and on. If an item is made in silver, Mayer's probably has it. These nice people also do replating of their customers' worn silverplate.

*PLUMMER McCUTCHEON / 145 East 57th Street between
Lexington and Third Avenues / second floor of Hammacher
Schlemmer / Monday through Saturday 10:00 to 6:00 / 421–1600*

Plummer McCutcheon carries silverplated tea and coffee services. Their specialty, however, is a bamboo-pattern stainless steel place setting dipped in gold. It's sold in sets for eight of sixty pieces for about $150.

*JAMES ROBINSON / 12 East 57th Street between Fifth and
Madison Avenues / Monday through Friday 10:00 to 6:00,
Saturday 11:00 to 5:00 / 752–6166*

James Robinson's, best known for its antique silver (primarily 18th-century English and Irish), carries many hallmarked pieces of impeccable quality, both new and old. If you're a connoisseur of old rare pieces, Robinson is known internationally for its collection; if they don't have that special piece by Paul De Lamerie (c.1700), or the pair of Charles I bowls (c.1600), they will scout the dealer's market for you. If your preference is for fine reproductions, Robinson's has its own line of eighteen patterns of sterling silver flatware, handmade in England. Some of their patterns date back to 1691, when the business was founded. They can make special sizes and alternate patterns, and will vermeil their own things.

*TIFFANY & CO. / 727 Fifth Avenue at 57th Street / third floor
Monday through Saturday 10:00 to 5:30 / 755–8000*

Tiffany only puts its name on sterling silver that has been made in its own factory. The Tiffany stamp is a guarantee of classic, heavy, well-made flatware, with a five-piece place setting starting at $119.75 and going up to $205.50. All silver made by Tiffany is sterling—no silverplate here—though they will vermeil their own pieces. Candelabra, coffee and tea sets, salt and pepper shakers, picture frames, bar accessories, Revere bowls, trays, ice buckets, commemorative calendars and practically anything that can be made in silver is made by Tiffany—including some amusing pieces that belie their "establishment" image. After all, there's nothing stodgy about a sterling silver shovel or a sterling silver tooth paste-tube winder.

*S. WYLER / 713 Madison Avenue at 63rd Street / Monday through
Saturday 9:00 to 5:30 / 838–1910*

S. Wyler carries many fine old pieces of silver and some that's old, not so fine, but still very usable (see page 9).

Sports

Athletic equipment is becoming increasingly sophisticated and, therefore, more and more stores are becoming specialists in particular areas, such as riding, skiing and tennis. For convenience we've separated the specialists from the all-around shops.

GAMESMANSHIP STORES

There are three stores that care about all sports and carry a full range of goods for archery, badminton, baseball, boating, bowling, boxing, camping, exercising, fishing, football, golf, hockey, hunting, paddle tennis, Ping Pong, tennis, shooting, skating, skiing, swimming, squash and—well, we may have failed to mention it, but chances are they haven't failed to stock it.

ABERCROMBIE & FITCH / Madison Avenue at 45th Street
Monday through Saturday 9:15 to 5:45 / 682-3600

GERRY CROSBY & CO. / 3 Pennsylvania Plaza on 31st Street
between Seventh and Eighth Avenues / Monday, Tuesday,
Wednesday 9:30 to 6:00; Thursday and Friday 9:30 to 8:00
563-6464

HERMAN'S / 135 West 42nd Street between Broadway and Sixth
Avenue / Monday through Saturday 9:00 to 7:30 / 730-7400

To The Hounds

Three shops in our town cater particularly to the horse and (not incidentally) to the rider. They carry "correct" equestrian apparel and equipment for English, race, polo, dude ranch or Western riders. You'll find English and Western boots, as well as crops, hats, breeches and jackets. If it's saddle soap you're after, most of them have that, too. Tally ho!

H. KAUFMAN & SONS SADDLERY CO., INC. / 139 East 24th Street between Lexington and Third Avenues / Monday through Saturday 9:00 to 5:45 / 684-6060

M. J. KNOUD / 716 Madison Avenue between 63rd and 64th Streets Monday through Friday 8:30 to 5:00, Saturday 8:30 to 4:00 838-1434

MILLER HARNESS COMPANY / 123 East 24th Street between Lexington and Park Avenues / Monday through Friday 9:00 to 5:30, Saturday 9:00 to 4:30 / 691-1000

Jogging Along

Even serious joggers, running for their lives, now want their feet to be stylishly and, of course, comfortably shod as they do their miles. Most department stores now carry shoes for joggers but N.Y., N.Y. is probably the only city that has whole stores devoted to the needs of the feet of the athlete. Favorite jogging places are the East Side and Riverside Drives, and around the reservoir in Central Park.

ATHLETE'S FOOT / 170 West 72nd Street between Amsterdam and Columbus Avenues / Monday through Saturday 10 to 9 874-1003

Whatever your Walter Mitty sports dream, Athlete's Foot has the shoe for you. They have shoes for women, for men (up to size 17), and for children (starting from size 10). Run, rabbits, run.

RUNNER'S WORLD / 275 Seventh Avenue at 26th Street
    Monday through Friday 10:00 to 6:00, Saturday 10:00 to 5:00
    691–2565

This sporting goods store is a bit off the beaten track, but it is a great place to buy all kinds of running shoes. Fairly good ones cost about $20, but beginners, who need better support, are advised to get more expensive models.

Ski Bums and Bunnies

Both Bloomingdale's and Saks Fifth Avenue have good ski shops for ski clothes. Bloomie's shop, however, is open only from August to January. The shops that specialize in skiing equipment, not only for the back, but for the slopes as well, are listed below. In these shops you'll find all the famous American and European brands of ski clothes, plus a wide range of equipment: skis, bindings, poles, boots, and even wax and goggles. The selling staffs are mostly dedicated skiers themselves, so if you are a beginner they can put you on the right track, and if you are a long-time schusser you'll appreciate the service department, which can save you precious time when you finally arrive in snow country. At Post Ski and Sport they even supply the practice slope—well, anyway, they have a machine called a Ski-Deck.

POST SKI AND SPORT / 1323 Third Avenue between 75th and
    76th Streets / Monday through Friday 10:30 to 7:00, Saturday
    10:30 to 6:00 / 744–5104

SCANDINAVIAN SKI SHOP / 40 West 57th Street between Fifth
    and Sixth Avenues / Monday through Friday 9:30 to 7:30,
    Saturday 9:30 to 5:30 / 757–8524

Tennis Anyone?

The three places listed below can equip you for the game with everything, with the possible exception of a good backhand and a court. Tennis Lady, as the name implies, caters just to ladies and carries marvelously different clothes (many of their own design), but no tennis rackets. The other two shops cater to both men and women and carry socks, tennis shoes, elbow and wristbands, headbands, hats, skirts, dresses, shorts, shirts and warm-up suits. They also have many brands of new rackets, and will restring your old one.

FERON'S RACQUET AND TENNIS SHOP / 55 East 44th Street between Madison and Vanderbilt Avenues / Monday through Friday 8:30 to 6:00, Saturday 9:30 to 4:00 / 867-6350

THE RACQUET SHOP / 289 Madison Avenue between 40th and 41st Streets / Monday through Friday 8:30 to 6:00, Saturday 10:30 to 4:30 / 685-1954

TENNIS LADY, INC. / 765 Madison Avenue between 65th and 66th Streets / Monday through Friday 10:00 to 6:00, Saturday 10:00 to 5:30 / 535-8601

PLACES FOR ACTIVE SPORTS

In our High Rise City, there are an amazing number of oases for active sports. Before setting out to any of the facilities listed, it is wise to call to inquire about hours, days, fees, guest privileges and membership requirements, if any.

Riding

CLAREMONT RIDING ACADEMY / See page 103.

Skating Rinks

LE PETIT / See page 56.

ROCKEFELLER CENTER RINK / See page 56.

SKY RINK / See page 56.

WOLLMAN RINK / See page 56.

Tennis Courts

BOULEVARD GARDENS / 51–26 Broadway, Woodside, Queens Monday through Sunday 7:00 to 8:00 / 545-7774

CENTRAL PARK TENNIS COURTS / West 93rd Street / daily 10:00 to dusk; summer, daily 7:00 A.M. *to dusk / 348–9884*

CITY TENNIS COURTS / permit required / general parks information: 360–8196

TENNIS PORT INC. / 51–24 Second Street, Long Island City for members only / 392–1880

PLACES FOR SPECTATOR SPORTS

The Yankees, Mets, Rangers, Knicks and Jets play in New York. Tickets for their games are available at their arena box offices and through Ticketron (see page 207). The N.Y. Giants are no longer New Yorkers and so do not qualify for this book.

Home of the N.Y.:

KNICKS AND RANGERS (Basketball, New York Knickerbockers; Hockey, New York Rangers) Madison Square Garden, 4 Pennsylvania Plaza, Seventh Avenue between 31st and 33rd Streets 564-4400

METS AND JETS *(Baseball, New York Mets; Football, New York Jets) Shea Stadium, 126th Street and Roosevelt Avenue, Queens 672–3000*

YANKEES *(Baseball, New York Yankees) Yankee Stadium, 161st Street and River Avenue, Bronx / 293–6000*

Sporting Pictures and Prints

The greatest collection of Currier and Ives prints are at the Museum of the City of New York. A great collection of Remington art can be seen on the walls of the "21" Club. Neither group is for sale, so if you are in the market for art for den walls, the two sources below will provide a lot for you to see and buy.

KENNEDY GALLERIES, INC. / 40 West 57th Street between Fifth and Sixth Avenues / fifth floor / Tuesday through Saturday 9:30 to 5:00 / 541–9600

The sportsman and nature lover will find a flock of American paintings, prints and sculpture from the 18th, 19th and 20th centuries at Kennedy. The gamut runs from Frederick Remington paintings to hunting-dog prints.

SPORTSMAN'S EDGE / 136 East 74th Street between Lexington and Park Avenues / Monday through Saturday 10:00 to 6:00 249–5010

Mecca for the sportsman who absolutely craves prints and oils for his study or den. This is the specialist for fishing and hunting scenes, endangered animal species . . . they're all here. They print some of their own editions and issue a yearly catalogue.

Stationery

The style in stationery today is not stationary. True, the pure cotton stock, beautifully engraved from Tiffany and Cartier, is still a staple of the best-dressed desks, but now there are a hundred other ways to express yourself on paper. Papers that are chic today.are ordinary plain brown wrapping, recycles, rice, onion skin, graph and color, color, color. You can buy paper cut to size and then have it bound into pads, monogrammed (by embossing, engraving or imprinting), and bordered in contrasting colors. Bloomingdale's, Bonwit's, Saks Fifth Avenue and virtually every other department store has its own lines of note paper and desk impedimenta.

HENRI BENDEL / 10 West 57th Street between Fifth and Sixth Avenues / Monday through Saturday 10:00 to 5:30 / 247-1110

A totally nontraditional approach to stationery and invitations is what you'll find in Bendel's stationery department. Its Paper Shop carries cards in lively colors and interesting trims. Huge scratch pads, ready for imprinting, are one of its specialties.

BERGDORF GOODMAN / 754 Fifth Avenue at 58th Street main floor / Monday through Saturday 10:00 to 6:00, Thursday 10:00 to 8:00 / 753-7300

Bergdorf Goodman has its own exclusive designs for those who want to personalize Christmas cards. The good-looking bordered cards with matching envelopes leave plenty of room for your own greeting. And when February 14th draws nigh, the antique Valentine cards here will captivate any heart. The stationery department also stocks a complete line of paper, cards, note pads and invitations by Crane and others.

DEMPSEY & CARROLL / 38 East 57th Street between Madison and Park Avenues / Monday through Friday 9:00 to 5:30, Thursday 9:00 to 6:30, Saturday 9:00 to 5:00 / 486-7500

Dempsey & Carroll do the fastest and some of the finest engraving in town on invitations, playing cards and matches. They carry a good selection of Crane paper and are excellent at designing monograms for an entire wardrobe of classic, beautiful stationery. They also stock a wide variety of informals from which to choose.

FOLIO 72 / 888 Madison Avenue between 71st and 72nd Streets
Monday through Friday 10:00 to 5:30 / 879–0675

This attractive stationery boutique stocks reams of whatever paper, pads and cards are just hot off the presses. They will imprint almost anything you want on almost any paper stock. (They do stop short at a paper handkerchief.) Here you'll find other desk accessories—pencils, pens, blotters, etc.

FULLER STATIONERS / 45 East 57th Street between Madison
and Park Avenues / Monday through Friday 10:00 to 5:30
688–2243

This stationery store's speciality is office supplies. Fuller has a full color range of typing paper and index cards, and will imprint stationery, envelope flaps, stick-on labels, rubber stamps. In fact, it carries all the tools of the secretary's trade.

GROLAN STATIONERS / 115 West 57th Street between Sixth
and Seventh Avenues / Monday through Friday 9:00 to 6:00
247–2676

Grolan has a comprehensive stock of office supplies and will make deliveries.

HALLMARK GALLERY / 720 Fifth Avenue at 56th Street
Monday through Saturday 9:30 to 6:30 / 489–8320

The Hallmark Gallery carries an enormous variety of traditional greeting cards for every occasion, in addition to invitations, thank-you cards, place cards, and note cards with matching envelopes.

MRS. JOHN STRONG / 699 Madison Avenue between 62nd and
63rd Streets / Monday through Friday 8:30 to 4:00; open for short
time on Saturday; consultation with Mrs. Strong by appointment
only / 838–3775

Mrs. Strong is the lady who designs many of the fabulous papers sold in stationery shops such as Folio II and Bendel's. You can buy directly from Mrs. Strong, though the price will be the same as at the shops that sell her products, but you do get her personal attention and superb creative advice for any special items you care to have made to order. Call for an appointment.

Taxis

Most taxis in New York are painted a bright yellow. Each of these cabs is licensed and every driver is required by law to display his photograph and license on the dashboard of his cab. Taxicabs have meters, which the driver must activate for every trip. Drivers must take the passenger to airports or anywhere in the City, with the passenger responsible for paying all tolls. It is customary to give the driver a tip of approximately 15% above the total on the meter. (Unlicensed cabs, or "gypsies," also circulate on the streets. They are not regulated as to price, driver, insurance, etc. Neither are they yellow.)

There are two ways to get a cab in New York when there's no doorman around to flag one for you. The first and most usual method is to stand on a corner and hail one. If the roof light is on, the taxi is free (unless there is another lit sign saying "Off Duty" or "On Radio Call"). If the top lights are off, the taxi is in use.

Sometimes, however, it is more convenient to telephone a cab company, especially when it is raining or snowing. For either method, allow extra time when a taxi is needed between the hours of 8:30 A.M. and 9:30 A.M. and between 4:30 P.M. and 7:30 P.M., as these are the rush hours. All companies listed below are open seven days a week, twenty-four hours a day.

ALL CITY RADIO TAXI / 3009 Heath Avenue, Bronx / 796–1111

DIAL-A-CAB / 2104 Avenue X, Brooklyn / 743–8383

DING-A-LING / 534 Hudson Street, New York City / 691–9191

MINUTE MEN / 25–17 41st Avenue, Long Island City / 937–7000

SCULL'S ANGELS / 31–11 126th Street, Corona / 457–7777

Tickets

The New York newspapers and magazines are the most accurate references for what is playing where and when. Tickets for all events can be purchased at cost by writing, or visiting, the individual box offices.

There is a kiosk right in the center of Times Square, Broadway and 47th Street actually, at which you can buy tickets for some theatrical productions on the same day as the performance, at reduced prices. This office opens at 3:00 P.M. (Wednesday, Saturday and Sunday, noon to 2:00, for matinee tickets). It is officially known as the Times Square Theatre Center.

Tickets may also be purchased through ticket brokers, whose charges vary from 75¢ to $2.50 per ticket added to the box office price.

ACE THEATER / 153 West 55th Street at Seventh Avenue / Monday through Saturday 10:00 to 6:00 / 247-7373

Ace adds $2 to the price of each ticket.

BLOOMINGDALE'S / Lexington Avenue between 59th and 60th Streets / Monday and Thursday 9:45 to 9:00, Tuesday, Wednesday, Friday, Saturday 9:45 to 6:00 / 223-7278

On the mezzanine of Bloomingdale's you can get tickets for all events at Lincoln Center (except those at the Vivian Beaumont Theater). Their fee is 75¢ above the box office price.

MANHATTAN TICKET SERVICE / 1501 Broadway between 43rd and 44th Streets / Monday through Saturday 10:00 to 6:00 582-3600

Manhattan's service charge is $2 above the price of the ticket.

JACK RUBIN / 1560 Broadway at 46th Street / Monday through Saturday 10:00 to 5:00 / 354–3000

Tickets obtained by Jack Rubin carry a $2.50 additional fee.

DAMON RUNYON MEMORIAL / 33 West 56th Street between Fifth and Sixth Avenues / Monday through Friday 9:30 to 5:00 582–5405

Ask for Betty! She can get tickets to almost any Broadway show and have them waiting at the theater box office in your name. In return, you pay the box office price and make a tax deductible contribution to the Damon Runyon Memorial Fund of between $10 and $20, depending on the demand for the tickets. (All charges must be paid in advance at the Damon Runyon Memorial office.)

TICKETRON / Executive Offices: 1350 Sixth Avenue at 55th Street for ticket information: 977–9020
Ticketron Outlets: *Grand Central Station, Lexington Avenue at 42nd Street, Macy's, Broadway and 34th Street*

Tickets bought through Ticketron must be picked up at their outlets. Their charge above the box office price is 75¢ per ticket.

Tobacconists

~~~~~~

ALFRED DUNHILL OF LONDON / 620 Fifth Avenue at 50th
  Street / Monday through Saturday 9:30 to 5:30 / 684–7600

Alfred Dunhill is a typical tobacconist. In this shop there are fifty
different blends of pipe tobacco from which to choose. Records are
meticulously kept of customers' preferences so that re-orders and gifts are
easily available. You can spend anything from $10 to $70 per pound for
Dunhill blends. They also carry cigars, cigarettes and their famous
Dunhill lighters.

NAT SHERMAN CIGARS / 711 Fifth Avenue at 55th Street
  Monday through Saturday 9:30 to 6:30, Sunday noon to 5:00
  751–7818

Nat Sherman will brand his cigarettes with your name. He carries ten
different blends of cigarette tobacco, which he will wrap in the paper
color of your choice. A pack of twenty with plain wrappings costs $1.25.
He also carries pipe tobacco and cigars.

"21" CIGARS / "21" Club / 21 West 52nd Street between Fifth and
  Sixth Avenues / Monday through Saturday noon to 12:30 A.M.
  closed Saturday May till September / 582–7200

The "21" Club carries twenty (what, not "21"?) different kinds of cigars.
The price range is 25¢ to $1.25. Also, "21" will keep valued customers'
valued cigars locked up in their humidors on the premises.

Travel

Most airlines have ticket offices in Manhattan so that you can deal with them directly, if you know where you want to go and when. Travel agencies can be invaluable, however, for trip planning that involves changing airlines, making connections, booking hotel reservations, etc. Many special-interest group trips emanate from New York for travelers who do not want to go it alone. Generally, there is no charge to the customers for the agency services; the fees are paid by the companies who reap the profits.

AGENCIES

LINDBLAD TRAVEL, INC. / 133 East 55th Street between Lexington and Park Avenues / Monday through Friday 9:00 to 5:00, by appointment / 751-2300

Lindblad is known for its specially arranged group tours. Most of their trips take you to off-the-beaten-track places. For example, one tour concentrated on hunting artifacts in Afghanistan. This travel planner has brochures which detail every aspect of its tours, from the time you leave to your return, so that you know exactly what you're getting into.

PORTS OF CALL TRAVEL / Saks Fifth Avenue's Luggage Shop East 49th Street between Fifth and Madison Avenues / second floor / Monday through Friday 10:00 to 5:30 / 752-2446

Port of Call is run by two very savvy women who really have been to almost every corner of the globe and know which corners are the nicest or most undiscovered. If it's a very special trip you want, whether to the Amazon or down the Nile, they will be delighted to help. They also plan trips of the nonexotic variety just as efficiently.

VACATION ASSOCIATES / 342 Madison Avenue between 43rd and 44th Streets / Monday through Friday 9:00 to 5:00
661-2510

E.B. Miller and his Vacation Associates will plan any trip for you, giving you the same courteous service whether you're going to Boston or Brussels.

AIRLINES

All major airlines fly into N.Y., N.Y., which makes it easy to book your own reservations; but for complicated itineraries, reserving hotel rooms, renting cars and other special arrangements, going via a travel agent is even easier. For your convenience, major airline telephone numbers are listed below; for the names of travel agents we use, see above.

One of the great services in and out of our City's La Guardia Airport is the Eastern Airline Shuttle. These no-frill flights leave hourly for Boston and Washington, D.C.; no reservations are required and you can even buy your ticket on the plane.

For all flights, except the Shuttle, check to see from which airport your plane departs. New York is serviced by three major airports: La Guardia, JFK (Kennedy) and Newark. Bus and limousine services are available for all three; any passing taxi will deliver you, but a bit more expensively. When traveling independently to the airport from midtown, allow about one half hour to get to La Guardia, one hour to travel to Kennedy or Newark, and more for all three during morning and afternoon rush hours.

AEROFLOT SOVIET AIRLINES / 661-4050

AEROLINEAS ARGENTINAS / 757-6400

AERONAVES DE MEXICO (Aero Mexico) / 391-2900

AIR CANADA / 421-8000

AIR FRANCE / 759-9000

AIR INDIA / 751-6200

ALITALIA AIRLINES / 582-8900

ALLEGHENY AIRLINES / 736-3200

AMERICAN AIRLINES / 661-4242

AVIANCA AIRLINES / 586-6041

BRANIFF INTERNATIONAL / 687-8200

BRITISH AIRWAYS / 687-1600

BRITISH WEST INDIAN AIRWAYS / 581-3200

CHINA AIRLINES / 581-6500

DELTA AIRLINES / 239-0700

EASTERN AIRLINES / 986-5000

EL AL ISRAEL AIRLINES / 486-2600

FINNAIR / 889-7070

IBERIA AIRLINES / 793-3300

ICELANDIC AIRLINES / 757-8585

IRISH INTERNATIONAL AIRLINES (Aer Lingus)
    575-8200

JAPAN AIRLINES / 759-9100

KLM ROYAL DUTCH AIRLINES / 759-3600

LAN CHILE AIRLINES / 582-3250

LUFTHANSA / 357-8400

NATIONAL AIRLINES / 697-9000

NEW YORK AIRWAYS HELICOPTER / 661-5100

NORTH CENTRAL AIRLINES / 581-8851

NORTHWEST ORIENT AIRLINES / 564–2300

OLYMPIC AIRWAYS / 838–3600

OZARK AIRLINES / 586–3612

PAN AMERICAN AIRLINES / 973–4000

PIEDMONT AIRLINES / 489–1460

QANTAS AIRLINES / 800–227–4500

SABENA BELGIAN WORLD AIRLINES / 961–6200

SCANDINAVIAN AIRLINES / 657–7700

SWISSAIR / 995–8400

TAP PORTUGUESE AIRWAYS / 421–8500

TRANS WORLD AIRLINES / 695–6000

UNITED AIRLINES / 867–3000

VARIG BRAZILIAN AIRLINES / 682–3100

VIASA VENEZUELAN INTERNATIONAL AIRWAYS
421–7722

TRAINS

There are two major rail terminals in N.Y., N.Y., Grand Central (Lexington Avenue and 42nd Street) and Penn Station (32nd and Seventh Avenue), so if your plans include a journey by train, these are the numbers to call for information and reservations.

Train Information

AMTRAK / 736–4545

NEW JERSEY COMMUTER LINES (CON-RAIL) / 736–6000

TRAINS FROM GRAND CENTRAL STATION
532–4900

Train Reservations

> *Reservations for AMTRAK,*
> *METROLINER, AMTRAK PULLMAN: 736-4545*

Umbrellas

Department stores and specialty shops, such as Gucci, Mark Cross and Hermès, carry umbrellas—some are expensive, some not so. In these places you can buy rainbow-hued golf umbrellas, plastic bubbles, the classic black English bumbershoots, collapsible Knirps, sterling-silver-handled French parasols and "everybody whose anybody's" signature umbrellas. Still, with all those umbrella sources, illegal sidewalk vendors spring up like mushrooms everytime it rains on every New York corner, offering their own nameless brands of rainproofing. If you look over every umbrella offered and still can't find the right one, we have one more place for you to look— the ultimate:

UNCLE SAM / 660 Lexington Avenue between 55th and 56th Streets
Monday through Friday 9:00 to 5:45, Saturday 10:00 to 5:00
755-3553

Uncle Sam's collection of umbrellas is multitudinous and splendiferous. If you want to match a dress or coat, or even color-scheme your golf umbrella, he will be your "spoke" man and make it to order.

Wallpapers and Paints

There are dozens and dozens of wallpaper designers in New York. Generally, their works are displayed either in showrooms at 979 Third Avenue or in shops around that area. The reason famous wallpaper designers such as Hannett and Morrow, Schumacher, Margowen, Patterson, Piazza and Scalamandre are not listed here is that their wares must be ordered through a decorator or a retail store. One of the places, in addition to department stores, where you can see some of their samples is listed below.

JANOVIC/PLAZA / 1292 First Avenue between 69th and 70th Streets / Monday through Friday 7:30 to 6:30, Saturday 9:00 to 6:00 / 535–8960

This is a wholesale and retail wallpaper and paint house. Janovic/Plaza is the one-stop place to see dozens of books full of wallpaper samples from many different manufacturers. In the paint department they have the best color selection in the City and will mix the House and Garden (or any other) colors for you on the spot. If you have a decorator's card you will get the standard discount when you order your wallpaper or choose your paint. And if you're a retail customer you'll get the same fine service decorators get.

Watches and Clock Shops

There are shops within most of the department stores that carry watches such as Sesame Street's Cookie Monster, Timex, and more expensive timepieces made by Porsche and Baume & Mercier. There are also, in our town, many fine jewelers who give their own names to watches and clocks. In this case, the mechanism is generally bought elsewhere and enclosed in cases and faces and bands of the jeweler's own design. Sometimes these shops also carry a few of the famous name timekeepers.

Cartier, Tiffany and Van Cleef & Arpels carry their own private label clocks and watches, as well as some of the better-known brand names. David Webb carries only his own. We have sorted out for you special shops where timepieces are the "mainsprings" of the business.

BUCHERER, INC. / 730 Fifth Avenue between 56th and 57th Streets / Monday through Saturday 10:00 to 5:30 / closed Saturday during August / 757–8140

At Bucherer's you'll find their own brand, plus Baume & Mercier, Piaget and Rolex. They also repair watches, but only the brands they carry.

GÜBELIN / 745 Fifth Avenue between 57th and 58th Streets / Monday through Saturday 10:00 to 5:30 / closed Saturday July and August 755–0053

The fine watches that Gübelin carries, in addition to their own, are Audemars, Piaget, Omega and Patek Philippe.

LYON'S BULOVA ACCUTRON CENTER / 339 Madison Avenue between 43rd and 44th Streets / Monday through Friday 9:00 to 5:00, Saturday 10:00 to 4:00 / 661–6810

At Lyon's you can see a huge variety of Bulova clocks and watches, including their Bulova Accutron and Caravelle. They also do repairs on the premises.

TOURNEAU / 500 Madison Avenue at 52nd Street / Monday through Saturday 9:30 to 6:00 / 758–3265

Tourneau, the watch and clock specialist, carries Rolex, Accutron, Omega, Patek Philippe, Tourneau and Le Coultre.

Wines and Spirits

There are hundreds of liquor stores in midtown Manhattan. Since prices are about the same everywhere, as is the speed of delivery service, the only thing that truly differentiates liquor dealers is the breadth and depth of their wine selections. Depending upon clientele, vendors stock domestic and imported wines from the cheapest to the finest, and some vendors stock both.

EMBASSY LIQUORS, INC. / 796 Lexington Avenue between 61st and 62nd Streets / Monday through Saturday 9:00 A.M. to 10:00 P.M. / 838–6551

A neighborhood store that has all liquors, some fine French wines and a big selection of less expensive Italian, Portuguese, Spanish, Chilean and domestic wines, including some N.Y. State vintages. Speedy deliveries.

*PARK LANE / 16 East 58th Street between Fifth and Madison
Avenues / Monday through Saturday 8:00* A.M. *to 9:00* P.M.
753–5160

Although Park Lane is small and not very fancy, it carries all the
necessities and most of the exotics. Very cooperative and fast with
deliveries, including their already chilled white wines.

*QUALITY HOUSE / 2 Park Avenue at 32nd Street / Monday
through Friday 9:00 to 8:00, Saturday 9:00 to 7:00 / 532–2944*

The selection of wines and liquors at Quality House lives up to the
name. They sell both by bottle and by case and will special order
anything you want if they do not have it in stock.

*SHERRY-LEHMANN, INC. / 679 Madison Avenue at 61st Street
Monday through Saturday 9:00 to 7:00 / 838–7500*

This is one of the great wine and liquor stores in town. If you are a true
oenophile, browse here and make your selection. If you are a novice, you
can rely on their knowledgeable salespeople. You will get the same
courteous service if you select a Romanian wine at $1.99 or Le Paradio
Ragnaud Cognac at $350. Sherry sells wine and liquor by the bottle and
by the case, and makes up attractive gift packages.

*VENDOME LIQUEUR, INC. / 12 East 45th Street between Fifth
and Madison Avenues / Monday through Friday 9:00 to 6:30,
Saturday 9:00 to 5:30 / 753–2595*

A very attractive shop, whose owner particularly cares about wine. Often
he discovers a little-known vintage that's very, very kind to the palate
and to the pocketbook.

Zoos

See page 52.

HAVE FUN!

ABOUT THE AUTHORS

CHARLOTTE / Charlotte Ford was Michigan born, but New York bred. The elder daughter of Henry Ford II, she has shopped the world over and now lives in N.Y., N.Y. with her daughter Elena. In 1976, she introduced a collection of clothes that carries her name. She brings to the book her knowledge of how to live and bring up a child in The Big Apple.

ISABELLE / Isabelle Russek Leeds is the only native-born New Yorker among the authors. Her vocation is politics, her avocation is shopping. She serves as N.Y. Governor Hugh L. Carey's Special Assistant for International and United Nations Affairs. It is her special pleasure in the line of duty to help the diplomatic community in the joys of New York living.

PHYLLIS / Phyllis Cerf Wagner is a transplanted Okie who has lived her entire adult life in New York. Her multifaceted career has encompassed advertising, writing a newspaper column and book publishing. She was married to the late Bennett Cerf and is presently Mrs. Robert F. Wagner.

SUSAN / Susan Payson Fine is a down-easterner from Maine who made her way in New York as the director of Public Relations for a major Fifth Avenue department store. She is married to cosmetic executive William Fine, and stylishly keeps homes in New York, in Connecticut, and in Ireland.